GOING
FROM
BASIC
TO C

ROBERT J. TRAISTER

Prentice-Hall, Inc., Englewood Cliffs, New Jersey 07632

Library of Congress Cataloging in Publication Data

Traister, Robert J. (date)
    Going from BASIC to C.

    Includes index.
    1. C (Computer program language) I. Title.
II. Title: Going from B.A.S.I.C. to C.
QA76.73.C15T694 1985   001.64'24   84-42959
ISBN 0-13-357799-6

Editorial/production supervision: **Karen Skrable Fortgang**
Interior design: **Jayne Conte**
Cover design: **Whitman Studio, Inc.**
Manufacturing buyer: **Anthony Caruso**

LIMITS OF LIABILITY AND DISCLAIMER OF WARRANTY

The author and publisher of this book have used their best efforts in
preparing this book. These efforts include the development, research, and testing of the theories and programs to determine their
effectiveness. The author and publisher make no warranty of any
kind, expressed or implied, with regard to these programs or the
documentation contained in this book. The author and publisher
shall not be liable in any event for incidental or consequential
damage in connection with, or arising out of, the furnishing,
performance, or use of these programs.

Printed in the United States of America

10 9 8 7 6 5

ISBN 0-13-357799-6 01

PRENTICE-HALL INTERNATIONAL, INC., *London*
PRENTICE-HALL OF AUSTRALIA PTY. LIMITED, *Sydney*
EDITORA PRENTICE-HALL DO BRASIL, LTDA., *Rio de Janeiro*
PRENTICE-HALL CANADA INC., *Toronto*
PRENTICE-HALL OF INDIA PRIVATE LIMITED, *New Delhi*
PRENTICE-HALL OF JAPAN, INC., *Tokyo*
PRENTICE-HALL OF SOUTHEAST ASIA PTE. LTD., *Singapore*
WHITEHALL BOOKS LIMITED, *Wellington, New Zealand*

To Rayburn and JoAnn Hickerson

CONTENTS

PREFACE

This book is written especially for the BASIC language programmer who is contemplating or presently making the switch to C language. The reasons for learning to program in C are many. These include the increased flexibility of the language, the speed of execution, and the fact that C has been called the best possible language available today for microcomputers. Without a doubt, it is very advantageous to know how to program in C. The portability of this language from machine to machine means that once you know how to program in C, you can bring most of your programs up on nearly any microcomputer for which a C compiler is available.

BASIC programmers seem to have the most difficulty in making the transition to C. There are many reasons for this, but possibly the most prevalent one is the lack of printed information designed especially to help BASIC programmers make the transition. In the past, C has been the tool of the system-level programmer and software designer. In other words, C has been more or less restricted to the world of the professional programmer. On the other hand, BASIC enjoys popularity in nearly every field of computer programming.

If you know how to program in BASIC and are capable of using most or all of the statements and functions available in this language, moving up to C should not present tremendous difficulty, provided you have the right instruction. The C language "Bible" is *The C Programming Language* by Brian W. Kernighan and Dennis M. Ritchie. These authors were intimately involved in the development of C. However, even the advanced BASIC programmer will probably have a great deal of difficulty sifting through the information presented in their book. The reason for this is that the audience for which this book was written was devoid of BASIC programmers. The book was never meant to be a tutorial, but rather a reference manual to C.

However, once you are introduced to C through a proper tutorial, this book becomes an invaluable aid.

Going from BASIC to C is an introductory tutorial and reference guide specifically for BASIC programmers who are making the transition from BASIC to C. This book contains a large number of BASIC programs and their C language program equivalents. Hopefully, this book will serve as a reference guide to programmers who are more accustomed to thinking in BASIC than in C. By seeing specific BASIC programs and their close or exact C language counterparts included in these pages, the reader should gain a quicker and better grasp of C because the latter is taught in the environment of BASIC, a conventional reference point for all BASIC programmers. It is the hope of the author that this text will make your transition from BASIC to C a pleasant learning experience.

Robert J. Traister

ACKNOWLEDGEMENT

The author would like to acknowledge and thank Lifeboat Associates, Inc. for supplying the Lattice C-Compiler (Version 2.0) to be used as a model for this book. Additionally, this company provided technical assistance at every step of the way.

INTRODUCTION

If you are a BASIC programmer just starting out in C, or a BASIC programmer who has no experience whatsoever with C, this book is written for you. *Going from BASIC to C* will take you step by step through that part of C which will allow you to (a) begin writing simple programs in C; (b) fully understand the relationship between BASIC statements and C functions; and (c) build up an adequate knowledge base in order that you may comfortably and effectively use higher-level C instructional manuals.

C has been described as the best language for microcomputers. C compilers are available for many types of microcomputers, and most work in close conjunction with the original C language developed by Bell Laboratories approximately ten years ago. While C is adaptable to most computers, one does have to choose a model system in preparing a book on C. For this book, the following system and software were used as the model:

1. Lattice C-Compiler
2. IBM Personal Computer with 320K memory
3. 2-360K Diskette Drives
4. IBM Monochrome Display and Adapter
5. IBM Color Graphics Card
6. Princeton Graphics Systems HX-12 RGB Color Monitor
7. IBM Dot Matrix Printer

This by no means stipulates that this same system be used to run programs in this book. C is a very portable language, and all programs discussed in this text follow the standard C language format and use the standard set of C functions. Chances are that any system you use and any compiler that contains the full C language will be adequate to compile and run the sample programs.

It is not even necessary for you to be set up to run C language programs. While it is quite helpful to be able to input the program examples and observe the test run, the information contained in this book is an adequate introduction to the world of C without your having to run a single C program. This is true because this text uses many BASIC language programs (written in Microsoft BASIC) as a reference source.

The reader is encouraged to experiment with modifications of the C language programs described and not to move on to a new section until the previous section is fully absorbed. I think you will find your transition from BASIC to C a useful and challenging one, one which will not be fraught with a great deal of misunderstanding.

C PROGRAMMING LANGUAGE

C programming language is a relatively new language developed by Bell Laboratories. It has been called the most up-and-coming language among high-level program developers due to its small size, economy of expression, and general-purpose programming attributes. But what is C? Most of its users term it a shorthand version of assembly language. The code is compact, and execution speed is very fast. C is somewhat of an oddity insofar as programming languages are concerned. It is not classified as a high-level language like Pascal, Fortran, COBOL, and BASIC. Yet, neither is it a low-level language on the order of assembly. C is often called a "relatively low-level language," a "high-level version of a low-level language," or even a "low-level version of a high-level language." It can probably be best described as a moderate-level language that falls midway between low- and high-level languages.

Traditionally, most C language programmers were former assembly language programmers who had little difficulty seeing the similarities of operation between the two languages. However, persons who were initiated into computers through a high-level language such as Fortran or BASIC sometimes have difficulty making the transition to C. This is especially true of BASIC language programmers.

However, C is a very compact language. The number of statements and functions contained in C is quite small, so it is not a difficult language to learn—not nearly as difficult as BASIC, for example. The difficulty in learning C often comes from prejudices that are naturally harbored by persons who learned to program computers in a high-level language. For example, the transition from BASIC to C is extremely difficult for many persons who have a high degree of expertise in BASIC. Since the great majority of nonprofessional microcomputer programmers are initiated into microcomputers through BASIC, this may be a major reason why the use of C has been relegated primarily to those programmers who are considered professionals; those who earn a living through programming.

The fact of the matter is that if microcomputer programming were taught to beginners by using both BASIC and C, the entire learning process might be quickened, and the programmer would be more inclined to adapt readily to other languages. The sad fact is that most microcomputer hobbyists who have the potential to move on to the professional level never do so because they become "stuck" in BASIC, and the relearning process is simply too difficult.

I'm certainly not dunning BASIC. It is a highly useful and powerful language, but, like all high-level languages, it is too structurally limited to allow most persons to branch outward and program functions that are unique, at least to BASIC.

Let me first assure you that C can do anything BASIC can. However, instead of the many capabilities of BASIC being directly available in C, the latter offers only the building blocks from which these same capabilities can be derived. To demonstrate this in a most simplistic way, the following program in Microsoft BASIC shows how the MID$ function can be built using other capabilities of Microsoft BASIC.

```
10 REM BASIC PROGRAM EXAMPLE
20 REM EMULATION OF MID$ FUNCTION
30 DIM A$(5)
40 A$(1)="H"
50 A$(2)="E"
60 A$(3)="L"
70 A$(4)="L"
80 A$(5)="O"
90 START=2
100 ND=3+START-1
110 FOR X=START TO ND
120 X$=X$+A$(X)
130 NEXT X
140 PRINT X$
```

The word "HELLO" is contained in an array (A$). In BASIC, we tend to disassociate string variables from string arrays. To the computer, however, they are just about the same. More appropriately, in this example, the computer thinks of A$ as a character array (alphabetic) that equals in total the word "HELLO." The MID$ function in Microsoft BASIC allows us to pull a certain portion from the string array. The actual characters removed or reassigned are determined by the values you use with MID$. Lines 90 through

130 are the equivalent of:

X$ = MID$(A$,2,3)

This indicates that we wish to assign to X$ the value of the second, third, and fourth characters in A$. For example,

X$ = A$(2)+A$(3)+A$(4)

Using standard Microsoft BASIC statements, line 90 assigns a value of 2 to numeric variable START. This marks the starting point of the MID$ assignment (the second character in A$). Numeric variable ND is assigned the offset value or number of characters that are to be removed from A$. Line 110 begins a FOR-NEXT loop that begins its count at START (equal to 2) and terminates when X is equal to ND + 1.

Line 120 uses X$ to take elements from the A$ array sampled by the FOR-NEXT loop. When the loop times out, X$ is now equal to MID$(A$,2,3). The remaining program lines simply print the total value of X$ on the screen. Lines 90 through 130 represent a subroutine that extracts the MID$ portion of A$. In C, the equivalent lines would be called a function that could indeed be named MID$. All this function requires is the insertion of the variables (called arguments). These would consist of A$, START, and ND. If Microsoft BASIC did not possess the MID$ function, it would be necessary for you to build such a function from the statements and/or other functions already available to you, assuming you needed this type of routine.

This is exactly the way C language works. It is a language that offers a limited number of statements and functions from which many, many functions can be built. Indeed, using C, we can build functions that can emulate all of the commands, statements, and functions available in BASIC.

At this point, someone will usually ask "Why?" If the MID$ function is so useful, why isn't it already included as one of the standard functions in C? The answer to this is that as useful as the MID$ function is for many text processing applications, it may not be exactly what the programmer is looking for. For instance, suppose you wanted a MID$ equivalent that will return the characters specified only if they are alphabetic. All numeric characters would be skipped over. The MID$ function in Microsoft BASIC does not allow this directly. By adding more program lines, you can cancel out the numeric characters that might be returned by MID$; but these extra program lines require more execution time and a larger program. In C, such a function could be programmed as easily as the standard MID$ function discussed previously. C, then, allows you to build functions that are custom-designed for a specific task. It precludes us from having to make do with preassigned functions that may not fully address our needs. And we can do this in a minimum amount of space, thus making programs far more compact and efficient with regard to program execution speed.

C language compilers are equipped with a limited set of standard C functions. While small in number, they are large in scope and can be used to build hundreds of thousands of other functions. This is done by combining the standard function capabilities. Each function is almost like a separate program in itself, which only needs to be fed the proper arguments to perform its task. This is the key advantage of a moderate-level language. Unlike assembly language (low-level), which accomplishes its purpose by building functions a bit or byte at a time, C is at a higher level. It allows us to do much of what can be accomplished in assembly language in a shorthand manner. Therefore, C is much easier to use, will run almost as fast, and doesn't impose nearly the limitations of a high-level language.

Most programmers eventually fall into their own special niche regarding the tasks they handle and the personal programming methods they use to accomplish these tasks. Likewise, a standard set of user-defined functions built from the standard C functions is created. These "personal functions" need only be programmed once and stored on diskette. They can then be called from other C language programs that must make use of their capabilities. To make comparisons in the simplest of conventional terms, we can say that a program is like a house. An assembly language house would be build from individual bricks, boards, pipes, and so on. A high-level language house would be built from large modular units that might include the roof as a single unit, the foundation as another unit, the walls as yet another unit, and so on. On the other hand, a C language house would be built from much smaller modules, such as framed doorways, paneling, sections of walls, and so on. The assembly language house gives us the absolute in flexibility, while the high-level language house provides the least. The C language house gives us much of the flexibility of the assembly language house, but at an increased building-time efficiency.

C LANGUAGE: A HISTORY

The development of C and the UNIX operating system is attributed by many to the competitiveness of a small group of programmers at Bell Laboratories in Murray Hill, New Jersey. This competitiveness would seem to be restricted to the individuals themselves, competing one against the other on a mostly friendly basis. Apparently, when they were building UNIX, one would take up where the other left off, then another, and so on, until the cycle was complete, and the first would start in again. This development has been described as a fermentation of diversified ideas. There was no lack of criticism among the developers regarding improvements. Naturally, the names Brian W. Kernighan and Dennis M. Ritchie come into the picture as members of this group, but another name stands out quite prominently: Ken Thompson, who was heavily involved in developing a Pascal program at the University of

California at Berkeley. He is described by many programmers as the best in the world, and no one will deny he is great. After leaving Berkeley, Thompson became involved in the MULTICS project, which was a joint venture of the Massachusetts Institute of Technology, the Honeywell Corporation, and Bell Laboratories. Bell later dropped out of the project, but MULTICS was eventually developed for the GE-465 computer and also for the Honeywell 6045. MULTICS provides its many users with a powerful means of managing and sharing files. The name MULTICS may have figured very prominently in naming the UNIX operating system. Ken Thompson's work with MULTICS before Bell dropped out had reached a point where he had written an editor called QED, which is still probably used to this day on MULTICS.

However, once Bell Labs and MULTICS were no longer associated with one another, Ken Thompson sought other avenues to fill the void. He was able to latch onto a DEC PDP-7, and in his spare time put together an operating system. It was written in assembly and was called UNIX. It is seriously presumed by many system-level programmers that the name UNIX stands for a castrated version of MULTICS. This may or may not be a fact, but UNIX was certainly designed along the lines of a single-user MULTICS—the first UNIX was a single-user version.

While it would appear that Thompson may have entered this project on a personal basis—and most likely alone—at some point in its development, he began to attract attention and quite a bit of interest. Somewhere during the development, Dennis Ritchie came in on the project. At about the same time, the UNIX operating system was transferred from the surplus PDP-7 to a surplus PDP-11. (In this context, surplus simply means the machines were not actively being used by Bell.)

As this sequence of events was taking place, Ken Thompson wrote an interpreter for a language called B, which is a language similar to BCPL, the latter being a portable language that made some rather simple assumptions about the machine on which it was operating. As a result, programs could be ported from machine to machine quite easily. A comparison today between BCPL and C would show a number of similarities. Thompson enjoyed the fact that code could be written in a fairly easy manner with BCPL and refined a portion of it to come up with B. The reason B was chosen as the name for this language is probably due to the fact that it was a very small and simple part of BCPL; therefore, the first letter of the mother language was chosen as its name.

When Dennis Ritchie entered the picture, he became interested in the interpreter that Thompson had written and ended up writing a compiler called C. The name was not chosen because C follows B in the alphabet, but because it is the second letter in BCPL, and the compiler he had written was a logical progression from this mother language.

Getting back on track, UNIX was now written in assembly language and was transferred to the PDP-11. One almost gets the impression that there was a race among this small group at Murray Hill to do something new and different with a system that had apparently sprung out of one man's fantasies. The next logical step was to rewrite UNIX in C. This was done, and it apparently did not take very long to make this conversion. Of course, UNIX was in single-user form, and even this was addressed. A multi-user UNIX was developed using a simple recording. When this new system was brought up, it ran rather quickly.

To further illustrate the competition alluded to earlier, it is rumored that about this time, there was a very strong competition between those at Murray Hill who were BLISS-oriented and the Dennis Ritchie people, who were C-oriented. BLISS is a complex language that consists of a tremendously large number of operators. The competition involved the writing of an optimal code for the PDP-11. As it turns out, BLISS probably won, but due to the competition, the C optimizer is classified as excellent by many programmers. Basically, C grew because it was an optimal way to use the PDP-11 and because it has an amazing simplicity and a high degree of expressiveness.

From a system-level programmer's standpoint, C is desirable because a few lines of C correspond to the same amount of code of assembler. In other words, one could judge overall program size by comparing codes, avoiding the possibility of one line of C code suddenly blossoming into thousands of lines of assembler. C allows the programmer to retain a feel as to how much code is being generated.

When C was first introduced, it was extremely rare to see anything as complex as an operating system written in a high-level language. This, of course, was the case with the final versions of UNIX, which were written almost entirely in C. You will recall that earlier versions were written in assembler. Certainly, some operating systems had partially been written in a high-level language, but the major portions, and particularly the device drivers, were written in assembler. Again, UNIX uses C almost entirely, and even the device drivers are written in this high-level language. At the time, this was highly unusual. The reason for the extensive use of C in UNIX was its efficiency and the fact that it allowed the programmer to rate constantly how well a particular programming problem was being tackled in terms of machine cycles.

Of course, all this discussion involves C and the system programmer. What about the average microcomputer user? Well, we cannot really say "average" because this individual is relegated entirely to a BASIC interpreter. How about those slightly above-average microcomputer programmers who may have expanded outward to a BASIC compiler, FORTRAN, Pascal, or even a COBOL compiler? How does C fit into the auspicious group who use personal computers? Again, I am speaking here of the person who is not employed as a programmer but who may use a personal computer either in business or at home. The answer: There is already a small underground movement of people who are writing many of their programs in C. Back on the systems level again, many of the commercial software producers are rewriting most of their offerings in C. This also applies to new offerings. Some professional systems-level programmers do admit to seeing limited usage of C among computer hobbyists. There are some problems, however. Most C compilers do not perform functions such as array bounds checking. This could be implemented, but in most cases, it is not. Of course, the main problem is that at present there is no good interpreter available for C. While the interpreter slows execution time, it does speed the time required to actually write and begin executing the program. There is a faction in the software industry that would like to see a C interpreter for various machines, but it is certainly not a top priority project at this time. This would not be a terribly difficult project, so the software could be made available at a reasonable price. However, while the language is becoming more and more popular among professional programmers, it is still a bit of a mystery to the average personal computer user. The demand is not there at the present time, but anything could happen in the future.

Will C become the standard programming language of tomorrow? The answers are many and varied. Some feel the answer is yes, while others say no. One individual I spoke with surmised that it would, but that it would certainly be improved upon. When persons ask what language they should learn to be most effective as a programmer, there is no real answer. C may come closer than all of the others for a very strange reason. While the language does have its faults, it generally does not teach bad programming habits, like some of the other high-level languages do out of necessity. Pascal is a good example of this. Of course, many professional programmers come down hard on BASIC for the same reason. One must realize, however, that these criticisms are usually leveled by persons who have what could be classified as an intimate understanding of computers. Most of these persons are capable of programming in the language of the machine itself; the rest of us are limited to human-oriented languages that make the going much easier but at the same time limit operations. Perhaps C is the happy medium between machine language and the true high-level language.

While BASIC provides reasonably good understanding of what is taking place regarding a typical human impression of a computer run, it really gives us no idea what's taking place on a machine level. For this reason, many high-level programmers become utterly confused after writing a few short lines in BASIC, because they are more accustomed to thinking of machine operations on a machine level rather than concentrating primarily on the commands that bring about the ultimate result.

It is to be hoped that this discussion has given you a bit of insight into how C came about. If even half of the bits and pieces of information that have filtered back to me are true, it would seem that C was not developed as a result of a major corporation's attempt to produce a highly salable commodity for a booming business and scientific market. Rather, it all started with a handful of highly professional programmers who at first "toyed" with the idea of a simple language that suited their needs and would provide few restrictions and the ultimate in machine compatibility. Nor did C grow from only one person. It grew from the minds and imaginations of a handful who were in friendly competition with each other. They practiced the fine art of one-upmanship and the entire industry benefitted. Unlike almost every other language popular today, C did not grow out of an industry need; rather, it blossomed from personal desire, a desire to come up with something better. One might say that C sprang from a collection of benign ego trips that pitted a handful of individuals against the rest of the computer world in an effort that saw the former trying to develop something that was better rather than bigger. While some may argue, many will aver that this small group was victorious.

2 THE LATTICE C-COMPILER

The model compiler used for research in writing this book was provided by Lifeboat Associates of New York City. The Lattice C-Compiler version 2.0 is currently the most popular C compiler offered for use with the IBM Personal Computer. This is the result of a complete C language compiler as opposed to some others that only recognize a subset of the original C language. There are a few differences between the original C programming language and that provided by the Lattice C-Compiler. However, for the most part, these can be ignored, especially for the type of programs presented in this book. Most of the differences were prompted by a desire to make the language both more portable and more comprehensible. In other words, for microcomputer users, these differences make this version of the C programming language more useful. I think you will find that all of the programs presented in this book conform exactly to the major C programming reference source, which is *The C Programming Language* by Kernighan and Ritchie (Prentice-Hall, Inc.).

While the model compiler is the Lattice C version from Lifeboat Associates, the model microcomputer for researching this book is the IBM Personal Computer. This machine contains two 360K double-sided disk drives, 320K RAM, and the standard IBM monochrome display adapter and monitor. The model machine also has many other options that do not directly relate to the use of C programming language and are therefore not listed here. The disk files included with the Lattice C-Compiler take up approximately 160KB of disk storage. This is a two-phase compiler (two-pass). Each phase has about 50KB of program section, and each requires a minimum of an additional 14KB of data area. While the IBM PC is available with the older 160KB disk drives, these would present a problem, although they would be workable. The compiler needs about 160KB of working memory in addition to that taken up by the DOS operating system itself. For readers who wish to try this compiler with their IBM PC, a minimum suggested configuration would specify one 320K disk drive (two preferred) and a minimum of 128K RAM. A single disk drive will increase the length of time it takes you to compile your C language programs, because you will constantly be pulling out one diskette and replacing it with another. In addition to the 160KB taken up by the files on the compiler diskette, you will also need to add the LINK.EXE file from the IBM DOS diskette as well as the EDLIN file from the same diskette. This will consume approximately 45KB more disk storage space. You must then add to this the additional space required to hold your original C program, the object program that is the output from the compiler, and, eventually, the executable program (.EXE), which will be the output from the linker. This is pushing a single 320K diskette to its limits, and there's nothing worse than going through a long compilation and linking process only to be presented with an error message indicating that your disk is full and the executable program cannot be written.

WRITING, COMPILING, AND RUNNING

If your previous experience with computers has involved only BASIC, chances are that you've been using a BASIC interpreter rather than a compiler. Put simply, an interpreter converts a program into machine language a line at a time. Once the set of instructions brought on by that single line is executed, the interpreter goes to the next line, interprets it, and proceeds to the next line. When your program is running, the interpreter is converting your program lines to machine language. This is the primary reason why interpreters are so slow as far as execution speed is concerned. It takes a certain amount of machine time to read the BASIC statement line, more time to convert this information and send it to the microprocessor as machine language instructions, and still more time for the microprocessor to do its job and then return control to the interpreter, which must then seek out the next line.

A compiler performs similarly, but only up to a point. The compiler does its job before the program is ever executed. Put very simply, the compiler works once the program has been input via the keyboard. This applies to any compiler, whether it be in BASIC, C, FORTRAN, or any other language. The compiler acts like the interpreter previously discussed, in that it grabs each line of code and converts it to a rough equivalent of machine language. However, you must remember that the program is not being executed at this point. Whenever a conversion is made while using a compiler, the object code (semi-machine language) is output to the diskette as a separate file. For example, if your C program is stored on diskette as PROGRAM.C, after the compiler has done its thing, a new file will exist in addition to this one, which might be named PROGRAM.OBJ. At this point, the compiler ceases to operate. It is now necessary to link the object module, or program, to functions not defined by the C program itself and are machine-dependent in order to bring about an executable file. This one would be named PROGRAM.EXE. When the object module is properly linked, the resulting file (PROGRAM.EXE) can then be run on your computer. Using the IBM Personal Computer, the IBM linker is a file contained on the IBM DOS diskette. Its sole purpose is to link object files with the machine's operating system to allow them to be executed. When the compilation process and the linking have concluded, the program is run by simply typing in its name. It is not necessary to also type in the .EXE extension. It is only after the linking process has been completed that a program is executable. You may now completely erase your original C language program file (PROGRAM.C), although you will probably want to keep it on hand so that you may list its contents. The PROGRAM.OBJ file may also be erased. The only file you need is PROGRAM.EXE, which was derived from the previous two. In other words, your original C program, after being compiled and linked, has served its purpose. It is one of the products that has produced an executable file that may be thought of as the machine language equivalent of your original C language program.

Using an interpreter, the conversion to machine language is made, but it is not stored as a separate diskette file. When an interpretive program has completed its run, you still return to the original high-level language version in current memory. This may be stored on a diskette file, but each time the file is loaded into current memory, the runtime interpretation process must begin anew for it to run. With a compiler, the interpretation or conversion process is done only once, and this results in an executable file that the machine understands without any interpretation whatsoever. The machine has to work harder to execute an interpretive program. It has to perform many different functions to properly send each line to the microprocessor in a form that it can understand. The executable file that is the result of a compiled program is already in a form which the microprocessor can understand, so the machine doesn't have to work as hard. This means the executable file program is run much more efficiently (that is, faster). Depending on the particular program, the improved execution speed can involve a factor of three to ten times the speed of a similar program run under an interpreter.

There are a few drawbacks, the main one being that it takes longer to test and debug a compiled program than the same type of program run under an interpreter. Using your BASIC interpreter, you can type in a portion of the program and then run it immediately to see what results. With a compiler, the program must be typed in, compiled, and linked before execution can begin. If there is an error, you must go back to the original program, make the necessary changes, compile it again, link it again, and then execute it. Another drawback lies in the disk space required to store executable files as opposed to program files run under an interpreter. To make a comparison, let's assume that you type in a program using a BASIC interpreter and store it to disk file. Let's also assume that this particular program requires 1800 bytes of storage. This is all the disk storage space that is required for the same program to be executed, again using an interpreter. Using a compiler, you would again type in the same program and store it to disk. The requirement would still be 1800 bytes. However, the object module which is written to the disk that is the result of this original program would typically be $2\frac{1}{2}$ to 3 times the size of the original. Let's say it consumes approximately 5KB. This object module must now be linked to other programs to produce an executable file. This latter file is the one that we're really after. When the programs contained by the linker are included with the object module that sprang from the original program, the executable file size may consume 20 or more times the file space of the original program. Again, 1.8KB is required for the original program, 5KB for the object module, and 36KB for the executable file. Assuming that you erase the original program and the object module, the disk storage requirement for this single executable program consumes 20 or more times the space required by the original. If the original program were only half the size of the one specified (900 bytes), the size of the executable file would not be affected appreciably, since most of its space was occupied by the programs to which the object module was linked.

From a practical standpoint, the increased storage requirement of compiled programs is not a serious drawback. This only means that you will need more diskettes to store the same number of programs when compared with an interpreter. One must remember that the extra file space is being occupied by program information equivalent (roughly) to that which is being supplied by an interpreter on an ongoing basis. The main reason for running a compiled program lies in the greatly enhanced efficiency of execution, resulting in a much faster execution speed.

The Lattice C-Compiler, as previously mentioned, is a two-pass compiler. The compiler diskette contains two files, LC1.EXE and LC2.EXE. LC1 is the first phase of the compiler, while LC2 makes up the second. Together, they make up the entire compiler. Each performs a portion of the compilation process, and each must be invoked by separate commands at the keyboard unless a batch processing file is used. This compiler package also contains a batch file (LC.BAT) to execute LC1 and LC2 in succession. Here is the way a program is compiled. First, the C language program is input via the keyboard. Using the IBM PC and IBM DOS, one invokes the line editor (EDLIN). The C program is typed in a line at a time. When you exit EDLIN, the file is automatically written to diskette. This file must have a .C extension, so when you invoke EDLIN while in DOS, you would simply type EDLIN PROGRAM.C and then press Enter. When you have finished the program and exit EDLIN, a file will be written to diskette containing this program, which will be named PROGRAM.C. To begin the compilation process, you now type LC1 PROGRAM. This invokes the first phase of the compiler, and when it finishes execution, it will write to diskette a file named PROGRAM.Q. Now type LC2 PROGRAM, and the second phase of the compiler will be invoked. The output from the second phase will be the object module, PROGRAM.OBJ. The PROGRAM.Q file is no longer there, since it is automatically erased just before the second phase of the compiler halts execution. At this point, the compilation process is complete, and the file PROGRAM.OBJ may now be linked to other modules to result in an executable file.

Using the IBM linker, you may now type LINK CS+PROGRAM, PROGRAM, ,LCS*. This is a shortened version. You can also simply type LINK and then insert the name of the program as you are prompted. The linking process combines another object module that is also contained on the C compiler diskette. Its file name is CS.OBJ. The above link command line links CS.OBJ with PROGRAM.OBJ. Following the commas, the program name will again appear. This means that the executable program is to have the same name as the object module (PROGRAM.OBJ). Two commas are then inserted, back to back. This simply indicates that you do not desire a separate map file. The last insertion is LCS, which is another file contained on the C compiler diskette. The linker assumes that the extension for LCS is .LIB (standing for library). The compiler diskette file LCS.LIB is then read. The library file contains the definitions for all of the C language terms used in writing your original program. This simply tells the linker what to do regarding the writing of code for the object module. When the linker has completed its execution, the executable file, PROGRAM.EXE, will be written to diskette.

While this whole process sounds rather complex, you can do everything with a single command. This means writing a simple batch processing file under EDLIN. I call mine C.BAT. The following batch processing program will allow you to completely compile and link a C language program using the Lifeboat compiler and the IBM linker provided all files are contained on the same diskette:

```
LC1 %1
LC2 %1
LINK CS+%1,%1, ,LCS
ERASE %1.OBJ
```

With this simple batch processing program, all that is necessary to completely compile and link a C language program and arrive at an executable file is to

---

*This discussion assumes use of the small memory model of the Lattice C-Compiler, Version 2.0.

type:

C (PROGRAM NAME)

This assumes that your batch processing program is named C.BAT. If your C language program is named FILER.C, all you need do is type:

C FILER

All the necessary compiling and linking processes will be carried out automatically. If you're using two disk drives, you may not wish to include the LINK.EXE file on the same diskette as the one that contains the compiler files. Assuming that the compiler diskette is in Drive A and the diskette containing LINK.EXE is in Drive B, you can change line 3 of the batch processing program above to automatically switch to the proper diskette (B) to access LINK.EXE. Line 3 should be changed to:

B:LINK A:CS+%1,%1, ,LCS

The rest of the program may remain unchanged. By the same token, you may wish to conserve disk compiler space by relocating your C library file (LCS.LIB) on a diskette in Drive B, along with the LINK.EXE file. At this stage, you would simply change line 3 to:

B:LINK A:CS+%1,%1, ,B:LCS

You may delete line 4 if for some reason you wish to retain the OBJ file. I usually erase this automatically during the linking and compilation process using line 4 of the batch processing program. For very long programs in C, compilation and linking can take several minutes. By committing all operations to a batch file, you can simply type in a single line and do something else while the various programs are being accessed to produce an executable file.

Discussing the Lattice C-Compiler further, file LC1 reads a C source file (the one you typed in using the line editor). This file must have a .C extension. Provided there are no fatal programming errors, an intermediate file with a .Q extension is produced. File LC2 then reads the intermediate file (created by LC1) and produces an object file. The .Q file is deleted by LC2 when its processing is complete. The .OBJ file then serves as the input to the linker in order to produce an executable program file. Two special files must also be involved in the linking process in addition to the .OBJ file. These special files are CS.OBJ and LCS.LIB. The file CS.OBJ must be specified as the first module on the link execution command. CS.OBJ defines the execution entry and exit points for any program generated using the Lattice C-

Compiler. The file LCS.LIB must be specified as the library. This can be done either in a batch file as previously noted or when you are prompted by the linker to give the name of the library file. This file defines all of the run-time and I/O library functions included as part of the Lattice C package.

There are many aspects that make the Lattice C-Compiler quite interesting, but these are explained thoroughly in the company's excellent documentation. When compiling and linking the C programs discussed in this book, the information provided in this chapter should be adequate to take you quickly from the C source file mode to a fully executable file. If you are using a different compiler and/or a different computer, these specific instructions may not apply, although I think you will find that the general principles presented in this chapter will guide you through the compilation and linking process. Again, it is not necessary to understand what each file in the compiler does. It is necessary only to know how to get from a C source file to an executable file in the shortest time possible.

The Lattice C-Compiler was used for researching this book, because it contains all of the functions and capabilities discussed in *The C Programming Language* by Kernighan and Ritchie. In other words, the Lattice C-Compiler contains the standard language set for C. However, if you do not have this particular compiler or the Microsoft C Compiler, which for all intents and purposes is identical to the Lattice C-Compiler, don't be dismayed. Throughout this book I have included programs that are neither machine- nor compiler-dependent. Most C compilers can process the programs presented in this book. Some compilers contain subsets of the original language. Many of these subset compilers do not support floating-point arithmetic. Therefore, any programs in this book that use floating-point numbers cannot be compiled. However, many readers will not yet have purchased a compiler and will do so after learning a bit more about C. To anyone, regardless of whether or not you have a compiler, the materials contained in this book are carried out in standard C language style. Therefore, you should not be overly concerned about the compiler at this point, nor the machine itself. C is a portable language that was written especially to allow source programs to be transported to many, many different types of computers. If you learn the standard C programming language, you will be able to move easily into those areas that rely on a certain type of machine or compiler. For now, let's consider C to be universal and totally independent of anything other than the programmer's own knowledge and experience.

3 CONSOLE INPUT/OUTPUT CONVERSIONS

In computer terminology, the console or standard input/output names the monitor and the keyboard. The keyboard is the standard input device for a microcomputer, although others, such as the RS-232 port, diskette drives, and so on may serve as input or output devices. The programs listed in this chapter all receive information from the keyboard and output this information (often in modified form) to the monitor. These programs are representative of over 90% of the most common operations performed on computers.

The format for this chapter will hold true throughout. A BASIC program is presented and explained briefly. This is followed by the exact C language equivalent of the BASIC program, which is also explained on a line-by-line basis. By comparing the two programs, the reader should gain an immediate understanding of how the C program works and what functions in C duplicate the actions of statements and functions in BASIC.

PRINTING INFORMATION TO THE SCREEN

```
10 PRINT"COMPUTER"
```

This simple program uses the BASIC PRINT statement to display the quoted phrase "COMPUTER" on the monitor screen. This may seem like a simple, "one-action" program, but two discreet actions take place. First, the word "COMPUTER" is displayed at the current cursor position, but then, an automatic carriage return and line feed are effected on the screen so that the next cursor position will lie one row beneath the start of the word "COMPUTER."

C Language:

```
main()
{

        printf("COMPUTER\n");

}
```

This C language equivalent does exactly what the BASIC program did. It prints the word "COMPUTER" at the current cursor position and then returns carriage and advances the cursor to the next row. The printf function is the equivalent of PRINT in BASIC and is used very much like PRINT, at least when quoted phrases are used as the argument. In C, it is necessary to indicate that a carriage return and line feed are to be effected. This is done with the *newline character*, represented by the backslash n combination. Notice that the newline character is inserted within the quotation marks. This may seem unusual to a BASIC language programmer who is accustomed to seeing everything typed within quotation marks also printed to the screen. However, in C, the newline character is not printable. It simply triggers the newline action regarding the text cursor. One of the most common mistakes made by beginners in C language programming is to place the newline character outside the quotation marks. This will result in an error message during the compilation process.

BASIC Language:

```
10 PRINT"COMPUTER";
```

This is a close duplication of the previous program. However, a semi-colon has been added following the closing quotation mark, which indicates (in BASIC) that a newline character is not to follow the display of the quoted phrase. In BASIC, a newline character is assumed if the semicolon is omitted, as in the first program. This program will display the word "COMPUTER" starting at the current text cursor position. However, upon completion of the write, the cursor will remain on the same row and in the character position immediately following the "R" in "COMPUTER." The next screen write will begin at this cursor position.

C Language:

```
main()
{

        printf("COMPUTER");

}
```

This C language program does the same as the BASIC example. In C, if the newline designator (backslash n) is omitted, the text cursor is positioned one space past the last printable character on the same row. In BASIC, it is necessary to add a semicolon to omit the newline character, while in C, this is assumed. Without the semicolon in BASIC, the newline character is assumed.

BASIC Language:

```
10  X = 10
20  PRINT X
```

This program assigns the number 10 to numeric variable X. Line 20 uses the PRINT statement to print the value of numeric variable X on the screen. Since the semicolon following the PRINT statement line has been omitted, we know that the carriage return/line feed is in effect.

C Language:

```
main()
{

        float x;

        x = 10;

        printf("%f\n", x);

}
```

You may be surprised to see variable x declared a float in this C language program, but remember that each of these C language programs is to be an exact equivalent of the BASIC program. In BASIC, a variable is floating-point unless it is defined as an integer variable by a percent sign following the variable named, as in X%, or by using the DEFINT statement. In the

BASIC program example, variable X was assigned on integer value. However, it could also have been assigned a floating-point value. Therefore, X is a floating-point variable to which an integer value has been assigned. If line 10 had read:

10 X% = 10

variable x in the C language equivalent would have been declared int. Moving on, float x is assigned a value of 10 in the next line. Then printf is used to display this value on the monitor screen.

In this program, the conversion specifier %f is used to indicate to printf that it should look for a float argument, which is represented here by variable x following the quoted portion of the printf argument. Effectively, %f is replaced by the value of x.

BASIC Language:

10 PRINT 15

In this program, a constant is used with the PRINT statement. Whenever a numeric constant is used in this manner, it is printed directly to the screen just as if it were enclosed in quotation marks, although if it were, it would then become a string constant. Again, no semicolon follows this line, so the newline character is to be automatically generated.

C Language:

```
main()
{

        printf("%d\n", 15);

}
```

In this C language equivalent, the number 15 replaces the variable x in the previous C language example. Here, a constant is inserted directly as the argument. We already know that 15 is an integer. Therefore, the conversion specification %d is used to indicate to printf that it should be looking for an integer value. We could also have used %f, since an integer value can be accepted by a floating-point argument.

BASIC Language:

10   A$ = "COMPUTER"
20   PRINT A$

This example uses PRINT to display the value of a string variable on the monitor screen. Here, A$ is the variable and is assigned a value of "COMPUTER" in line 10.

C Language:

```
main()
{

        char *a;

        a = "COMPUTER";

        printf("%s\n", a);

}
```

Here, *a* is declared a string variable by using the char * declarator, or more accurately, a pointer to a string value. The variable is assigned the value of "COMPUTER" in the next line just as it was in the BASIC program. The printf statement line uses the %s conversion specification to indicate that a string value should be contained as an argument. Conversion specifier %s is replaced by the content of *a*, or more specifically, by the value that *a* points to.

BASIC Language:

```
10  A$ = "COMPUTER"
20  PRINT A$;
```

In this example, the value of A$ is to be displayed on the screen, but the semicolon in the program indicates that no newline character is to be generated. Therefore, the cursor will remain in the next cursor position following the letter "R" on the same row.

C Language:

```
main()
{

        char *a;

        a = "COMPUTER";

        printf("%s", a);

}
```

This program is almost identical to the previous C language example. The only difference is that the newline character has been omitted. This prevents an automatic carriage return and line feed from being generated. Incidentally, this program could also have been written using only a printf statement line without the declaration and assignment lines, as in:

```
printf ("%s", "COMPUTER");
```

This is exactly equivalent to:

```
printf ("COMPUTER");
```

BASIC Language:

```
10  B% = 12
20  A$ = "COMPUTER"
30  PRINT A$;B
```

This program prints the value of two variables, one a string type and the other an integer. The percent designation (%) following the B variable indicates that will always represent an integer value. Line 30 uses the PRINT statement to first print the value of A$, followed by the value of B. The semicolon that separates the two variables indicates that the second variable is to be printed on the same line as the first.

C Language:

```
main ()
{

        int b;
        char *a;

        b = 12;
        a = "COMPUTER";

        printf ("%s %d\n", a, b);

}
```

This program does the same thing as the BASIC version. Variable *b* is declared an integer, while *a* is declared a character string pointer. The next two lines make the assignments to *b* and *a*, respectively. The printf line uses two conversion specifications, %s for the string value and %d for the integer value. Notice that there is a space between %s and %d. Since this space is contained within the quotation marks, it is printed to the screen. This means that a single space will occur between the printing of the values of *a* and *b*. In BASIC, this is done automatically, as a space is inserted before and after a numeric value is printed, assuming other characters are printed before and after it. In C, however, it is necessary to specify this spacing, and this is done within the quotation marks. If the space were omitted, the two values would be printed as one. In other words, all characters would be sequential on the screen, with no spacing between the two different values.

BASIC Language:

```
10  A$ = "AGAIN"
20  PRINT"HELLO ";A$
```

This program prints the phrase "HELLO AGAIN" on the display screen. Notice that a space follows the "O" in "HELLO." This is done because BASIC does not automatically insert a space between two string variables used with the PRINT statement.

C Language:

```
main()
{

    char *a;

    a = "AGAIN";

    printf("HELLO %s\n", a);

}
```

This exact C language duplicate of the BASIC program includes the word "HELLO" within quotation marks, followed by a space and the string conversion specification, and finally, the newline character. The quoted word is displayed first, followed by the space and the value of *a*. Without the space, both words would run together. If you wanted to print the value of *a* first followed by the quoted word, you would change the printf line to:

```
printf("%s HELLO\n", a);
```

In this example, %s would be replaced by the value of *a*, followed by a space and the word "HELLO."

BASIC Language:

10 INPUT A%

The INPUT statement in BASIC temporarily halts execution until input is received from the keyboard. In this example, an integer is expected because of the percent sign (%) following numeric variable A. In response to this, if a floating-point number is typed in, it is converted to its integer value (that is, 1.494 = INT 1). The only legal value that can be successfully returned by this program is an integer.

C Language:

```
main ()
{

    int a;

    scanf ("%d", &a);

}
```

Here, the scanf function is used to read the keyboard. The conversion specification used with scanf (%d) indicates that scanf if to expect an integer input. Any other input is illegal and will not be accepted. The variable to which the keyboard input is assigned has previously been declared an int and is included as the argument for scanf. However, notice that this variable is preceded by an ampersand (&). The ampersand is required whenever scanf is used with a numeric variable. Scanf's arguments must always be pointers. The ampersand in front of the numeric variable indicates that it is a pointer, which tells where the input should be stored. After scanf is executed, variable *a* is equal to the integer input via the keyboard.

BASIC Language:

10 INPUT A%
20 PRINT A%

In this program, the INPUT statement asks for an integer to be input via the keyboard. This is assigned to variable A%. The PRINT statement line then displays the value of A% on the monitor screen.

C Language:

```
main()
{

    int a;

    scanf("%d", &a);
    printf("%d\n", a);

}
```

In the C language equivalent, *a* is again declared an integer, and scanf is used as before. The printf function line uses the %d conversion specification to indicate that an integer is to be displayed. This specification is replaced with the value of *a*. Scanf and printf are formatted in much the same manner, and it's easy to become confused. Scanf will never contain a newline character, and its argument will always be a pointer (numeric variables will be preceded by an ampersand). On the other hand, printf will often contain newline and other such characters, while its argument is not usually preceded by an ampersand.

BASIC Language:

```
10  INPUT A
20  PRINT A
```

This program allows INPUT to accept either an integer or a floating-point value. Since A is not followed by a percent sign, this means that it is a floating-point value.

C Language:

```
main()
{

    float a;

    scanf("%f", &a);
    printf("%f\n", a);

}
```

The C language equivalent is about the same as before. However, *a* is declared a float variable, and scanf and printf use %f conversion specifications. There is one difference in the displays resulting from this program when compared with the BASIC version. In BASIC, if an integer is typed via the keyboard, even though the variable can contain a floating-point number, an integer is displayed on the screen. However, in the C language version, an integer input will cause it to be displayed as an integer followed by a decimal point and a string of zeroes. In other words, the number is displayed in floating-point format even though there is no fraction. In most instances, this makes no difference whatsoever. This can be corrected, however. More about this later.

BASIC Language:

```
10  INPUT A$
20  PRINT A$
```

This program uses INPUT to retrieve a string value. This can consist of an alphabetic character, numeric characters, or alphanumeric characters. In other words, any input via the keyboard is acceptable (except for a comma). The input value is assigned to A$, and its value is displayed by the PRINT statement in line 20.

C Language:

```
main()
{

    char *a;

    scanf("%s", a);

    printf("%s\n", a);

}
```

Here, *a* is declared a string pointer, and scanf is used with the %s specification to indicate that a string is to be input. Notice, however, that the ampersand is not used prior to the variable in scanf. This is because *a* is already a pointer. It was declared a string pointer previously. All arguments used with scanf must be pointers. The ampersand preceding numeric variables causes these to be pointers, but with character string variables, the ampersand is not necessary because they are already pointers. This program can also be written in the following manner:

```
main()
{

    char a[40];

    scanf("%s", a);

    printf("%s\n", a);

}
```

In this example, a new type of declaration appears that has not previously been discussed. Here, *a* is declared a character array with a maximum of 40 elements. In C, character strings and character arrays can often be treated the same. Scanf can use either a character string pointer or a character array. Like string pointers, a character array variable is also considered a pointer, and no ampersand is required. We can also write this program in the following manner:

```
main()
{

    char *a;

    gets(a);
    printf("%s\n", a);

}
```

This program uses the *gets* function, which is a standard part of most C compilers available for microcomputers today. It was not discussed in the Kernighan and Ritchie manual, but it is quite similar to the getline function, which was discussed. The gets function stands for "get string" and accepts a string input from the keyboard. It will accept any keyboard character, including the comma (as will scanf). Like scanf, the argument for gets may be either a string pointer or a character array. No ampersand is used with these arguments.

BASIC Language:

```
10  A$ = "F"
20  PRINT A$
```

This program looks like several others already presented in this chapter, and in the context of BASIC, it is. In C, however, it can be written in a completely different form. The key to this BASIC program and its C counterpart lies in the fact that A$ is assigned a single character. In C, this can make all the difference in the world toward the goal of efficient programming.

C Language:

```
main()
{

    char a;

    a = 'F';

    printf("%c\n", a);

}
```

In this program, *a* is declared a char value as opposed to a character string pointer or char array. This means that *a* will be used to hold a single character rather than a character string. We could use a character string pointer, which is the equivalent of what was done in BASIC; but it pays to be as efficient as possible. This program assigns *a* the value of "F." Note that the character itself is surrounded by apostrophes (rather than quotation marks). If a character string pointer (char *) had been used, the "F" would out of necessity be surrounded by quotation marks. The printf function line uses the %c conversion specification, which indicates that a character is to be displayed. Char variable *a* may be assigned any character in the computer's character set, although only those that are printable will actually be seen on the screen.

Throughout this discussion, references have been made to conversion specifications that are single lower-case characters preceded by a percent sign. Conversion specification is an appropriate name, because these can be used to perform actual conversions as the following program demonstrates:

BASIC Language:

```
10  X% = 65
20  PRINT CHR$(X%)
```

This program uses the CHR$ function in BASIC to convert the integer value of X% to its ASCII character equivalent in the computer character set. ASCII 65 is a designation for the letter "A." Therefore, this program will print the letter "A" to the screen.

C Language:

```
main()
{

    int x;

    x = 65;

    printf("%c\n", x);

}
```

Here, x is declared an int, meaning that it will hold an integer value. The actual value is assigned in the second executable line. The printf function line again uses the %c conversion specification. This means that a character is to be printed as opposed to a number. The end result is the ASCII character represented by the value of x is displayed on the screen. This program is the exact C language equivalent of the BASIC version. The conversion specification in itself takes the place of the CHR$ function in BASIC.

BASIC Language:

```
10   X$ = "A"
20   PRINT ASC(X$)
```

This program uses the ASC function in BASIC to return the ASCII code of the character contained in X$. We already know that the ASCII code for "A" is 65. Therefore, ASC(X$) will also equal 65. The number 65 is displayed on the screen.

C Language:

```
main()
{

    char x;

    x = 'A';

    printf("%d\n", x);

}
```

In this program, x is declared a char variable and is assigned the value of 'A'. The printf function line uses the %d conversion specification, which indicates that the character contained in x is to be displayed as an integer; thus, its ASCII equivalent. The number 65 is printed to the screen. Here, the %d conversion specification takes the place of the ASC function in BASIC. Incidentally, we can get rid of the assignment line in BASIC by simply using the program:

10 PRINT ASC("A")

The C language equivalent is

printf("%d\n, 'A');

In the C language version, both the declaration line and the assignment line can be omitted by using this printf modification. This is true because no variables are used in the program at all. Variable x has been replaced by the character constant "A."

While printf has been used to display information to the screen, there are other functions that will accomplish this, although not with the flexibility that printf provides. For single characters or character strings, the standard C functions putchar and puts may be substituted for printf. Several examples are shown below.

```
        main()
        {

                char c;
A               c = 'A';

                putchar(a);

        }


        main()
        {

                char *c;
B               c = "COMPUTER";

                puts(c);

        }
```

Program continues

```
main()
{

C         putchar('A');

}



main()
{

D         puts("COMPUTER");

}
```

Standard C functions puts and putchar can be used only with character strings and characters. They cannot be used to display numeric values that are not committed to character strings. Each time either of these functions is used, a newline character is automatically generated. The four programs shown here are exactly equivalent to the following four, which use printf for display purposes:

```
main()
{

        char c;

        c = 'A';

        printf("%c\n", c);

}



main()
{

        char *c;

        c = "COMPUTER";

        printf("%s\n", c);

}
```

Program continues

```
main()
{

    printf("%c\n", 'A');

}



main()
{

    printf("%s\n", "COMPUTER");

}
```

As you can see, putchar and puts are quite convenient to use whenever specific format conversions are not required. They take less time to input than equivalent printf functions, but again, the flexibility of printf is not provided.

Conversion specifications can also be put to good use as substitutes for the BASIC TAB function and to limit the number of characters printed to the screen. In an earlier discussion when printf was used to display a floating-point value, it was stated that even if the value assigned to a float variable was an integer, printf would display it as a float value. For instance, if the number 14 were assigned to a float variable, this value, when displayed by printf, might look like 14.000000. These zeroes may be deleted from the display by using a line such as:

printf("%.0f\n", x);

where x is 14. The conversion specification is preceded by ".0". This indicates that no characters are to be displayed after the decimal point. The above program line can be used to allow floating-point values to be displayed as integers, although if the value is less than 1, nothing will be displayed.

In many programs, it's neither necessary nor desirable to display floating-point values to more than one or two decimal places. The following program line can be used to display floating-point values to two decimal places only:

printf("%.2f\n", 3.16953);

When this line is executed, the value 3.16 will be displayed on the screen. The remaining decimal places are simply deleted from the display. No rounding takes place. The decimal places are simply not printed. No conversion takes place on the float value itself, only on how it's displayed.

BASIC Language:

10 PRINT 3*4

This BASIC program calls on the PRINT statement to display the value of 3 times 4. Here, a mathematical operation takes place before the value is printed. This program will print the number 12 on the screen.

C Language:

```
main()
{

        printf("%d\n", 3 * 4);

}
```

There is nothing unusual about this program. The conversion specification used with printf indicates that an integer value is to be displayed. The integer value is obtained from the argument near the end of the printf line. As in the BASIC program, this argument is a mathematical operation that multiplies 3 times 4. The number 12 is again displayed on the screen.

BASIC Language:

10 X% = 3
20 Y% = 4
30 PRINT X%*Y%

This is a repeat of the previous BASIC language program, except that the numeric values have been assigned to integer variables. The number 12 is again displayed on the screen.

C Language:

```
main()
{

    int x, y;

    x = 3;
    y = 4;

    printf("%d\n", x * y);

}
```

The C program matches the BASIC program by assigning values to integer variables. These variables are then used in place of constants in the printf line.

BASIC Language:

10 PRINT 3∗4;4.1/2.1;22.8∗1.01;12/3

This BASIC program prints the results of four different arithmetic problems side by side on the screen. The semicolon indicate side by side display, although the newline character is generated after the last problem is completed.

C Language:

```
main()
{

    printf("%d %f %f %d\n", 3 * 4, 4.1 / 2.1, 22.8 * 1.01, 12 / 3);

}
```

This program mimics the BASIC version. Note that four conversion specifiers are used, since four different values are to be displayed on the screen. The first value is an integer (%d), the next two are floats (%f), and the last is an integer. The newline character follows to indicate a carriage return and line feed. So far, performing mathematical operations with printf in C has closely followed the same format used in BASIC.

BASIC Language:

10 PRINT 3/4

When this program is run, the screen will display .75, the result of 3 divided by 4.

C Language:

```
main()
{

A        printf("%f\n", 3 / 4);              WRONG!!!!!

}
```

Program continues

```
main()
{

      printf("%f\n", 3.0 / 4.0);

}
```

B

Two program examples are given here. The first is the *wrong* way, but it illustrates an area where many beginning C programmers experience difficulty. The second program is correct. In BASIC, the division of 3 by 4 is automatically handled by floating-point arithmetic. However, in C, the arithmetic handling of constants will automatically be done by integer arithmetic unless some indication is given that a floating-point operation is to take place. In the first example (the incorrect one), even though the conversion specifier indicates a floating-point value, the computer still handles the division of 3 by 4 as an integer operation. The integer value of 3 divided by 4 is 0 (zero), and this is the value that is returned to the conversion specification. When handling constants, it is necessary to indicate floating-point operations by listing values as floats. While the numbers 3 and 4 are integers, the numbers 3.0 and 4.0 are floating-point values, at least as viewed by the computer. In the second program example, the correct answer will be garnered. It is not absolutely mandatory to insert the decimal point on both sides of the arithmetic operation. For instance, 3.0 / 4 will work just as well as or 3 / 4.0. However, it's a very good idea to get in the habit of using decimal points throughout an arithmetic operation to be performed on constants to insure that a floating-point value is returned. This problem comes to light when an arithmetic operation is performed on integers whose result is a floating-point value.

BASIC Language:

```
10   INPUT A$,X,Y%
20   PRINT A$;X;Y%
```

This program accepts user input from the keyboard and requires that three different values be typed in. The INPUT statement asks for a character string, a floating-point value (or integer), and an integer value. The three input values are displayed on the screen by the PRINT statement in line 20. Assuming that the values "COMPUTER," 1.414, and 18 are input, they will all be input at one time using commas as separators. Upon input of the last value, the ENTER key is pressed, and these values are committed to their appropriate variables. All three are then displayed by line 20.

C Language:

```
main()
{

        char *a;
        float x;
        int y;

        scanf("%s %f %d", a, &x, &y);

        printf("%s %f %d\n", a, x, y);

}
```

or:

```
main()
{

        char *a;
        float x;
        int y;

        gets(a);

        scanf("%f %d", &x, &y);

        printf("%s %f %d\n", a, x, y);

}
```

These programs will not work exactly like the BASIC program, but they indicate the standard method by which these operations are carried out in C. In the first C program, *a* is declared a string pointer, while *x* and *y* are declared as float and int, respectively. Scanf is then used with multiple arguments. The first conversion specifier indicates that a string is to be received from the keyboard. The second and third indicate a floating-point value and integer value, respectively. The keyboard inputs are assigned to *a*, *x*, and *y* in order. Note that the ampersand precedes each of the numeric variables, since it is necessary to access a memory location. Remember, the ampersand indicates the location of each.

With scanf, it is necessary to press ENTER after each value is input. In this example, the comma separators will not work as in the BASIC program. Therefore, you would type in the string value and press ENTER, type in the float value and press ENTER, and do the same for the integer value. When multiple arguments are used with scanf, it becomes the equivalent of several sequential INPUT statement lines in BASIC, each requiring you to push ENTER before proceeding to the next.

In the second program, *a* is declared as a string pointer (char *) and is used with the gets function rather than scanf.

BASIC Language:

```
10   INPUT"TYPE YOUR NAME";A$
20   PRINT A$
```

This program uses the optional prompt message capability of the INPUT statement in BASIC. When the program is executed, the INPUT statement will display the prompt on the screen, and execution will temporarily halt until keyboard input is obtained. As soon as ENTER is pressed, the keyboard input will be displayed on the screen.

C Language:

```
main()
{

    char *a;

    printf("TYPE YOUR NAME ");

    gets(a);

    printf("%s\n", a);

}
```

There is no single function common to C that allows for outputting a prompt message and inputting a value via the keyboard. In this example, the prompt is handled by a separate printf function, the input by gets, and the display of the input by another printf function. Note that the first printf function line does not contain a newline character. This means that the cursor will not be returned to the left side of the screen following the display of the prompt. The input assigned to *a* by gets will be displayed on the same row and to the right of the prompt. Remember, when input is requested by the INPUT statement in BASIC or by scanf or gets in C, the information typed via the keyboard will be immediately displayed on the screen. In these program examples, another line is added to redisplay the previously typed information. The C program is exactly equivalent to the BASIC program:

```
10  PRINT"TYPE YOUR NAME";
20  INPUT A$
30  PRINT A$
```

Naturally, you won't get the question mark prompt with the C language version, nor should it be necessary; but if you are a stickler for detail, change the first printf line to:

```
printf("TYPE YOUR NAME ?");
```

Now, a question mark will be displayed following the prompt message, because it is included as part of the quoted string in the printf line.

To follow standard C language format, it might have been best to replace the last printf function line with:

```
puts(a);
```

Often, gets and puts are used as a matching pair, as opposed to gets and printf. This is true only when the value retrieved by gets is to be printed to the screen and followed by a newline character. If you change the last printf line to the above, the program run will still be identical to the original C program, since in this example, the last printf line is exactly equivalent to puts(a).

BASIC Language:

```
10  INPUT A$
20  PRINT A$
```

This program is exactly the same as a previous program. However, the method in which it is to be used will be a bit different. Assume that this program follows a prompt that tells you to input a single character from A to Z. In other words, A$ is used to retrieve a single character instead of a character string. The single character will be redisplayed on the screen by the PRINT statement in line 20.

C Language:

```
main()
{

        int c;

        c = getchar();

        putchar(c);

}
```

In this example, getchar is the single character equivalent of gets. It is used to retrieve a single character from the keyboard. Variable c will be equal to the character. Actually, variable c will really be equal to the ASCII code of the character. You may find it strange that variable c is declared int instead of char. In fact, it could be declared char, and this will work fine in most cases. However, in C, chars are automatically converted to integers anyway. The real reason that c is declared int instead of char lies in the operation of the getchar function itself. When any input function is called, an interrupt is sent to your computer, which causes execution to halt until a character is input via the keyboard. If, for some reason, C is not able to effect this interrupt, getchar returns an integer value (usually -1). If variable c were declared char, it could accept any character that could be typed via the keyboard. However, it could not accept the -1 value. Therefore, variable c is declared int so that it can accept -1 should a malfunction occur. The C program shown is intentionally made as simple as possible for explanation purposes. However, when getchar is normally used, test lines are also added to the source program which take appropriate actions should c be equal to -1. This same type of malfunction return procedure is carried out with gets as well, although its variable must always be declared char.

In this program, variable c receives the value of a character typed via the keyboard. Only one character must be input before pressing ENTER. If you type more than one character, only the first character typed is assigned to variable c. Putchar is used to display the value of c on the screen. It is the equivalent of:

```
printf("%c", c);
```

So as not to be confused, remember that %c is a conversion specification that indicates a character is to be displayed. The c in %c has no name relationship with variable c. If the named variable were a, b, or any other letter, the %c specification would still remain the same.

BASIC Language:

```
10  A$ = INKEY$
20  IF A$ = "" THEN GOTO 10
30  PRINT A$
```

This BASIC program uses the INKEY$ variable to provide another means of input. When used in this manner, the character typed via the keyboard is not displayed upon typing it, but is assigned to A$. The character is displayed only when line 30 is executed. Since INKEY$ does not wait for a character to be typed via the keyboard, line 20 tests for the presence of a null (A$ = ""). A null is generated when no character is typed. When this occurs, line 20 detects this and branches back to line 10. One can think of INKEY$ as a variable that constantly indicates what's coming in from the keyboard, and this includes nothing. It is necessary to add a test line to the program to constantly loop INKEY$ until a valid character is received by this variable. Again, INKEY$ is a variable much like any other. It is difficult, however, in that it represents what is coming from the keyboard. We usually use INKEY$ to test for a specific character at the keyboard, but this is not mandatory. In any event, this program forms an exitable loop between lines 10 and 20. The loop continues to cycle until any key is pressed. It is not necessary to press ENTER, as any character is automatically assigned to INKEY$. Therefore, the ENTER key character is treated just like any other keyboard character. The keyboard sampling is so fast that as soon as any key is hit, the loop is automatically exited. You don't have time to press a character key and then ENTER. In every case, only a single character is returned to INKEY$ and, thus, to A$.

C Language:

```
main()
{

        int c;

        c = getch();

        putch(c);

}
```

There is no exact equivalent to the INKEY$ variable that is part of the standard C language function set. However, the getch function is close. Getch is used to retrieve a single character from the keyboard. It is like getchar in this respect. However, getchar requires that the ENTER key be pressed after the character is input, while getch returns the character automatically, letting the program proceed to other portions. Unlike UNKEY$, getch does not constantly return the status of the keyboard. When getch is executed, the program is temporarily halted until a character is typed via the keyboard. Upon pressing any key, execution resumes, and the character is returned to the getch variable (in this example, integer variable c). Again, c is declared an int rather than a char, because there is a possibility that -1 will be returned due to a malfunction. If, for some reason, getch is unable to activate the interrupt, c will have a value of -1.

The operation of getch is quite useful in setting up an equivalent of INKEY$ in C. It is not necessary to add an extra line to set up an exitable loop while waiting for a character to be typed. In this example, the C language program is actually less complex than the BASIC version.

The character contained in c is displayed on the screen using the putch function, which is a direct console write. We could also have used:

```
putchar(c);
```

or

```
printf ("%c\n", c);
```

Note: Functions such as getch, putch, putchar, and getchar are often included in separate function or macro files on the diskette that contains your C compiler. These functions are normally found in the standard input file, usually called STDIO.H. To use them in a program, it is necessary to indicate to the compiler that the STDIO.H file is to be included in program compilation. The normal means of doing this is to use the #INCLUDE preprocessor command, as in:

```
#include "stdio.h"
```

This line will be found at the beginning of the program preceding the call to main( ). Consult your compiler manual to find out exactly where these input/output functions are contained.

SUMMARY

This chapter has dealt exclusively with the most common input and output functions in C. Most persons begin learning C with the printf function and then move on from there. However, it's usually only months later that printf is fully explored. It is a very powerful function, which can literally perform wonders when properly utilized in C language programs.

The scanf function is the input equivalent of printf. It is just as versatile in regard to accepting input from the keyboard. Both functions follow the same programming format. Their versatility lies in the fact that they can be used as input/output functions for any type of values or variable declarations available in C.

Both printf and scanf may be heavily used in many different types of C language programs. Any program that requires displaying of information and inputting of information from the keyboard will make use of these functions. It is important that their uses be fully understood before proceeding further.

ASSIGNMENTS

1. Write a program in C that allows you to input a single character, a character string, an integer, and a float value, and then displays these values on the screen. Do this using a single scanf function and a single printf function.

2. Write a program in C that will convert the constant 16.889 to its integer value using a single printf line.

3. Write a program in C that will display the value 2.8196 to only three decimal places.

4. Write a program in C that will accept a character from the keyboard in INKEY$ fashion and then print the keyboard character returned twice.

CHAPTER 4

C LANGUAGE STATEMENTS

In C, constant reference is made to functions and statements. Most of the elements we deal with in C are classified as functions until they are used within a program. When a function is terminated by a semicolon (;) within the executable body of a C language program, it then becomes a statement.

C does have a number of pre-built statements. The standard C language statements are:

if
if else
while
do while
for
switch
case
default
break
continue
return
goto

Many of these statements should be familiar to you. As a matter of fact, *if*, *if else*, *while*, *for*, and *goto* work in very much the same manner as they do in BASIC. The other statements are specially set up for the various C language routines they address.

Before addressing these statements, a brief discussion on logical operators is necessary. In BASIC, IF-THEN statements often include a number of logical operators. As a matter of fact, these operators may be used with other statements as well to shorten overall programming time. These logical operators are also available in C, but they are represented a bit differently. Also, logical operators are broken down into two discrete categories: logical connective operators and bitwise operators. Logical connective operators will be discussed first. These include AND and OR. In BASIC, these operators may also be used for manipulation of bits in binary numbers; but this is not the case in C.

The logical connective operators AND and OR are expressed in C language programs by the symbols "&&" and "||" respectively. As bitwise operators, they would be expressed as "&" and "|" respectively.

Another set of operators that are relied heavily upon in BASIC (and in all other languages as well) are the relational operators. These include the equals sign (=), more than (>), less than (<), more than or equal to (>=), less than or equal to (<=), and not equal to (<>). In C, many of these same operators apply, although there are some differences.

For instance, in C, the equals sign (=) is used as an assignment operator only. As an example:

```
a = b;
```

uses the assignment operator to assign the value of b to a. However, if we wish to compare the value of a with b and do something if the two are equal, the assignment operator (=) no longer applies. A BASIC program portion such as:

```
50   B = 75
60   A = B
70   IF A = B THEN (do something)
```

would be written in C as:

```
b = 75;
a = b;
if (a == b)
(do something);
```

This is a nonsense program (in both BASIC and C), but it illustrates the difference between the assignment operator (=) and the equality operator (==). They both mean something completely different. In the C language program portion, the assignment operator (=) is used to assign to variable b the value of 75 and in the next line to assign to variable a the value of b. However, in the *if* statement line, the equality operator (==) is used. We can say that the equality operator is used whenever two values are to be compared (as opposed to one or the other being changed). In C, "=" and "==" have two completely different meanings. The first makes an assignment; the other makes a comparison.

Going one step further, the BASIC program line:

100   IF A = B AND C = D THEN (do something)

would be written in C as:

if (a == b && c == d)
(do something);

In this example, the use of the two equality operators compares *a* with *b* and *c* with *d*. The connective operator "&&" takes the place of AND in the BASIC program. Both programs state if *a* is equal to *b* *and* *c* is equal to *d*, then do something. This means that both expressions on either side of the logical connective operator must be true for the action to take place.

Here is another example:

100   IF A = B AND C = D OR E = F THEN (do something)

The C language equivalent line would be:

if (a == b && c == d ‖ e == f)
(do something);

Both programs perform an action if *a* is equal to *b* and *c* is equal to *d*. If one or the other of these expressions is not true, but *e* is equal to *f*, the same action will be performed. If *e* is not equal to *f*, but the other two expressions are true, the action is still performed. To put it simply, the logical connective operators work in C just like they do in BASIC. One does have to be careful of the equality operators to avoid some very sticky problems. For example, if the C program line:

if (a = b && c = d)
(do something);

were used, the action (do something) would take place every time. Instead of comparing *a* with *b* and *c* with *d*, this line would assign *a* to *b* and *c* to *d*. Such mistakes are common among programmers who are making the switch from BASIC to C (and even to those of us who feel we have successfully made the switch), but after a while, one begins to more or less think in C as opposed to thinking in BASIC and converting to C. As this transition takes place, problems such as these diminish in occurrence.

The inequality operator in BASIC is represented as "<>". In C, the inequality operator is "!=". Therefore:

100 IF A <> B THEN (do something)

would look like:

if (a != b)
(do something);

in C.

The remaining relational operators in C match those in BASIC. But be careful! In C, the more than or equal to operator must be expressed in exactly that order. More than comes first, followed by equals. In BASIC, the more than or equal to operator may also be written as equal to or more than. This is not legal with most C compilers. The following list shows what is legal and what is not:

LEGAL:

>=   More than or equal to
<=   Less than or equal to

ILLEGAL:

=>   Equal to or more than
=<   Equal to or less than

Some C compilers may recognize some of the illegal operators listed here, but many do not. Be on the safe side and always list all operators in standard C format.

The bitwise operators may be used only with integer values in C and are listed below:

&   bitwise AND
| bitwise inclusive OR
^   bitwise exclusive OR
<<   left shift
>>   right shift
~   one's complement (unary)

They must not be confused with their logical connective counterparts. The following programs demonstrate the use of the bitwise operators:

BASIC:

100   X = 7 AND 1

C:

x = 7 & 1

For bitwise manipulations, the AND operator is used just like a connective operator in BASIC. However, in C, the bitwise AND operator is represented by "&", while the connective operator is represented by "&&".

With all of this in mind, we are prepared to move on to a discussion of many of the C language statements and their relationships to similar BASIC language statements.

BASIC Language:

```
10  INPUT X%
20  IF X% = 14 THEN PRINT "THAT IS THE NUMBER"
30  END
```

This simple program uses the INPUT statement to receive an integer value from the keyboard. If the value is equal to 14, a message will be printed; if not, the program terminates. The END statement is optional in this particular case, since BASIC will automatically stop execution when there are no more lines to execute.

C Language:

```
main()
{

        int x;

        scanf("%d", &x);

        if (x == 14)
                printf("THAT IS THE NUMBER\n");

        exit(0);

}
```

In this program, variable x is declared an int, while scanf assigns the keyboard input to the memory location of x. The *if* statement is used to test for the occurrence of x being equal to 14. Note that the equality operator (==) is used as opposed to the assignment operator (=). The statement that immediately follows is executed when the *if* test proves true (non-zero). The exit function is then executed. Its argument is zero (0), which is unimportant most of the time. This argument is returned to whatever function called exit in the first place (in this case, main()). In C, a value of -1 indicates a malfunction, while a value of 0 usually indicates all is well. The value of the argument really makes no difference at all in this application. Most of the time, you will see exit functions used with arguments of 0.

BASIC Language:

```
10  INPUT X%
20  IF X% = 14 THEN PRINT "THAT IS THE NUMBER":PRINT "I WAS
    LOOKING FOR"
30  END
```

This is a slight modification of the previous BASIC program. Here, multiple operations are carried out when the IF-THEN test proves true. The first phrase is printed to the screen, followed by the printing of the second phrase. The program then terminates when line 30 is executed. If X% is not equal to 14, nothing is printed, and the program is terminated.

C Language:

```
main()
{

    int x;

    scanf("%d", &x);

    if (x == 14) {
        printf("THAT IS THE NUMBER\n");
        printf("I WAS LOOKING FOR\n");
    }

    exit(0);

}
```

This program is quite similar to the previous C program, but more than the extra printf line has been added. Note that at the end of the *if* statement

line, there is another opening brace (pointing left). This is necessary when
more than one statement is to be executed as a result of the *if* statement
test. As stated earlier, whenever there is an opening brace, there is always a
matching closing brace. This one is found following the last printf line. Following standard C format, it is printed one line below the last statement line
and directly beneath the calling function or statement (in this case, *if*). All
statements that lie between the opening brace and the closing brace are executed when *x* is equal to 14. A brace may be used when only one statement
is to be executed; but this is not required and was not done in the previous
program examples. The *if* statement always expects at least one statement to
follow. This is assumed. If more than one statement is to follow, the braces
are required. If the braces are not included for multiple statement quantities,
only the first statement (the function immediately following the *if* statement
line) will be executed as the result of the *if* test proving true. All the remaining lines will be executed as if they were not a part of the *if* test.

BASIC Language:

```
10  INPUT X%
20  IF X%>= 10 OR X% = 5 THEN PRINT "BINGO"
30  END
```

This program tests for the value of X% being more than or equal to 10
or being equal to 5. If either of these conditions is true (since the logical OR
was used), the word "BINGO" is printed.

C Language:

```
main()
{
    int x;

    scanf("%d", &x);

    if (x >= 10 || x == 5)
            printf("BINGO\n");

    exit(0);

}
```

This illustrates the use of the relational and logical connective operators with the *if* statement in C. Note that the brace following the *if* statement line is not included because only one statement follows. The exit function, like the END statement in BASIC, is optional in this particular program, since execution will automatically terminate when there are no more lines to execute. In C, a program is always ended by a closing brace that matches the opening brace following main(). This is the signal to terminate execution. Therefore, if the END statement were removed from the BASIC program, or the exit(0) function were removed from the C program, no run differences would be noted.

BASIC Language:

```
10  INPUT X%
20  IF X% = 22 THEN END
30  PRINT "TRY AGAIN"
```

While this program will run as is, it might be thought of as a portion of a BASIC program that terminates whenever X% is equal to 22, but does something else in other lines (not listed here) if X% is equal to anything but 22. When this program is run any number other than 22 will cause the prompt "TRY AGAIN" to appear on the screen. One might assume that a GOTO statement or another routine would follow line 30; but this is enough for our discussion. Here, the END statement in line 20 is extremely important, because it terminates execution of the program while there are still other lines that could be executed. In previous programs, the END statement was optional. In this one, however, it is mandatory.

C Language:

```c
main()
{
    int x;

    scanf("%d", &x);

    if (x == 22)
        exit(0);

    printf("TRY AGAIN\n");

}
```

This program does exactly the same thing as the BASIC version. The exit function is placed below the *if* statement line and is executed only when the value returned by scanf to x is equal to 22. Here, the exit function is mandatory for a successful program run.

LOOPS

Just as they do in BASIC, loops play an important role in C language programs. The best-known loop in BASIC is the for-next loop. Its equivalent in C is called a *for* loop. In BASIC, we can also loop with a WHILE-WEND statement. In C, the *while* loop does the same thing. C also boasts a *do-while* loop, which is not used very often, but which can be very useful in certain programming situations. In BASIC, we can also create loops that are continuous or exitable with the GOTO statement. C language also has a goto statement, but it is rarely used since there are so many more efficient ways of accomplishing the same thing with *while*, *for*, and *do-while*. The GOTO statement in BASIC is much used and abused. Most BASIC programmers would be lost without GOTO, but these same individuals may not take full advantage of the potential offered by the WHILE-WEND statement, which is rarely used. In C, however, the *while* loop is seen often; thus, gotos are seldomly used. Only in rare instances are gotos truly advantageous in C. The beginning C programmer should not rely too heavily on goto, since it may hinder his/her future development.

BASIC Language:

```
10   FOR X% = 1 TO 100 STEP 1
20   PRINT X%
30   NEXT X%
```

This is the standard FOR-NEXT loop demonstration program most BASIC programmers but their teeth on. Chances are, your first experience with a FOR-NEXT loop included a floating-point variable (X) rather than an integer variable (X%); but the two do exactly the same thing. From here on out, all BASIC variables will be declared integer variables by the addition of the percent sign (%) whenever they will hold integer values. This loop simply counts from 1 to 100 in steps of 1. The STEP portion is not necessary in this program, since without a STEP value, FOR-NEXT loops increment in steps of 1 as the default. However, this is not true in C, and the inclusion of STEP should make for a clearer explanation.

C Language:

```
main()
{

    int x;

    for (x = 1; x <= 100; x = x + 1)
        printf("%d\n", x);


}
```

The C language equivalent of the previous BASIC program uses the *for* loop. Within the parens following *for*, several statements follow. These are separated by semicolons that mark the end of a statement line. The first statement assigns x a value of 1. The second statement says that x is less than or equal to 100. The next statement assigns x a value of x plus 1. One can easily see the relationship between this portion of the C program and the FOR-NEXT loop in the BASIC program. This loop will count from 1 to 100 and increment x by 1 on each pass. Each time the loop cycles, the printf line is executed, and the value of x is printed to the screen. The first value of x determines the lowest value (in a positive stepping loop). The next value assigned to x in the *for* statement line assigns the maximum value to x. The last statement assigns the step value. Any statements that follow this line will be executed within the loop. If only one statement is to follow, no opening and closing braces are required to surround the executable state-ments. This is the case in this program. However, if more than one statement were to be executed in the loop, an opening brace would follow the *for* statement line, while a closing brace would be found at the end of the loop statements.

While this program is correct, it does not follow standard C language format in one respect. When a value must be incremented or decremented by itself plus or minus another number, it is not usually written as x = x + 1 or x = x - 1. To follow standard C language format, the *for* statement line should have been written as:

```
for (x = 1; x <= 100; ++x)
```

The notation ++x is exactly equivalent to x = x + 1. In a negative stepping loop, the notation --x is exactly equivalent to x = x - 1. This may seem a bit confusing at first, but as long as you know how these notations relate to what you've been doing in BASIC, you should have no problem. The notation ++x simply means that x is incremented by 1 each time this line is executed. The notation --x means that x is decremented by 1 each time the line is executed.

BASIC Language:

```
10   FOR X% = 1 TO 100 STEP 1
20   PRINT X%
30   PRINT X% + 10
40   NEXT X%
```

This is the same program as before, except that an extra PRINT statement has been added to display the value of X% plus 10. Two PRINT statements are executed within the loop, so two screen writes will take place on each of the 100 passes of the loop.

C Language:

```
main()
{

    int x;

    for (x = 1; x <= 100; ++x) {
          printf("%d\n", x);
          printf("%d\n", x + 10);
    }


}
```

This C language program also contains one extra statement within the *for* loop. Notice also that two extra braces have been added. The one immediately following the *for* statement line indicates that the following collection of statements is to be executed. The closing brace in the line immediately following the last printf line indicates the end of the statements that are to be executed within the loop. The last closing brace in the entire program marks program termination. This is the one that aligns with the opening brace that follows main().

To expand our knowledge of printf a little more, the C program could also have been written as follows:

```
main()
{

    int x;

    for (x = 1; x <= 100; ++x)
        printf("%d\n%d\n", x, x + 10);

}
```

Here, only one printf statement line follows the *for* line. Therefore, the extra braces are not required. However, the single printf line does exactly the same thing as the two printf lines in the previous C program. Note that in the printf line, two newline characters are included in quotation marks. The first conversion specifier, %d, is followed by the newline character. Therefore, the value of *x* is displayed, and a carriage return/line feed takes place. However, we're not yet finished with the contents of the printf line. Another conversion specifier is encountered. It is replaced with a value of x + 10. Still another newline character is generated. Remember, we can treat newline characters just like we do any other characters; but when they are printed, a carriage return/line feed takes place. Used effectively, they can greatly decrease overall program size when a great deal of formatted information must be printed to the screen.

BASIC Language:

```
10  FOR X% = 0 TO 100 STEP 2
20  PRINT X%
30  NEXT X%
```

This is a repeat of a previous BASIC program, except X% is incremented by 2 instead of 1 on each pass.

C Language:

```
main()
{

    int x;

    for (x = 0; x <= 100; x = x + 2)
        printf("%d\n", x);

}
```

The matching C language program is shown just to indicate that when the loop variable (or any other variable, for that matter) is to be incremented by more than 1 or decremented by more than 1, we revert to standard BASIC notation. Here, operations like ++x or − −x don't apply.

BASIC Language:

```
10  FOR X% = 100 TO 1 STEP –1
20  PRINT X%
30  NEXT X%
```

Here is the same routine shown earlier, except that X% counts from 100 to 1 in steps of - 1. When X% is less than 1, the loop terminates.

C Language:

```
main()
{

    int x;

    for (x = 100; x >= 1; --x)
        printf("%d\n", x);


}
```

The C language program is set up in much the same way as its BASIC counterpart. Since the loop is stepping in negative values, the first value assigned to x in the *for* statement line will be its maximum value. In this case, the value is 100. In the next portion of this line, the relational operator "more than or equal to" is used to indicate that the value of x will be more than or equal to 1. When this condition is no longer true, the loop will terminate. The notation − −x decrements x by 1 on each pass of the loop. I think you will agree that *for* loops in C are closely equivalent in format to FOR-NEXT loops in BASIC. Most programmers making the transition from BASIC to C experience little difficulty with *for* loops.

BASIC Language:

```
10 FOR X% = 1 TO 100 STEP 1
20 FOR Y% = 100 TO 0 STEP –1
30 PRINT X%;Y%
40 NEXT Y%
50 NEXT X%
```

This illustrates the use of a nested loop in BASIC. The X% loop is referred to as the outer loop, while the Y% loop is referred to as the inner loop. On each of the 100 passes of the outer loop (X%), the inner loop (Y%) will run through all 101 of its passes. I say 101 because Y% counts backward from 100 to 0 rather than from 100 to 1. On each pass of the Y% loop, the values of X% and Y% are displayed on the screen in horizontal format (side by side).

C Language:

```
main()
{

        int x, y;

        for (x = 1; x <= 100; ++x)
            for (y = 100; y >= 0; --y)
                printf("%d %d\n", x, y);


}
```

The C language version closely conforms to the BASIC version. There's nothing mysterious about placing a *for* loop within a *for* loop in C, although many readers may be wondering why an opening brace does not follow the first *for* statement line. It does appear that more than one statement is executed within the body of the outer (*x*) loop. In effect, there are two statements within the body of the outer loop. This includes the *for* statement and the printf statement. However, extra braces are not necessary because the outer loop really sees only the *for* statement. The printf statement line is associated with the *for* statement, which decrements y. In other words, when the nested *for* loop is executed, the printf statement is automatically associated with it. It is a single statement following a *for* loop. Therefore, no brace is necessary following the y loop. In fact, the printf statement is not really associated at all with the x loop. The only association with the x loop in this program is the y loop. In this usage, the entire contents of the y loop appear as one statement to the x loop.

BASIC Language:

```
10   FOR X% = 1 TO 100 STEP 1
20   FOR Y% = 100 TO 0 STEP −1
30   PRINT X%;Y%
40   PRINT X% + 10;Y% + 10
50   NEXT Y%
60   NEXT X%
```

This is the same program as before, except an extra PRINT statement line has been added within the body of the Y% loop. Each time the Y% loop cycles, the values of X% and Y% will be displayed, followed by these values plus 10. In this BASIC program, it is easier to see what I was alluding to in the explanation of the previous C program and the associativity of the statement contained within the y loop. Notice in the BASIC program that the two PRINT statements are enclosed within the Y% loop and bear no direct relationship to the X% loop.

C Language:

```
main()
{

    int x, y;

    for (x = 1; x <= 100; ++x)
        for (y = 100; y >= 0; --y) {
            printf("%d %d\n", x, y);
            printf("%d %d\n", x + 10, y + 10);
        }

}
```

In this program, braces have been added to enclose the multiple statements that are carried out within the body of the y loop. The x loop still sees the nested *for* loop as a single entity. Therefore, no braces are required to encompass the contents of the x loop, which effectively represent a single statement. The two printf statement lines are associated only with the y loop. Note that the closing brace for the y loop is located on the third line beneath the word "for," which opens the y loop. This makes it easier for anyone viewing the program listing to see exactly which statements are being executed by which calls. In this case, the contents of the inner braces are being called by the *for* statement.

BASIC Language:

```
10  FOR X% = 1 TO 100 STEP 1
20  FOR Y% = 100 TO 0 STEP -1
30  PRINT X%;Y%
40  PRINT X% + 10;Y% + 10
50  NEXT Y%
60  PRINT "CYCLING OUTER LOOP"
70  NEXT X%
```

Here is another program that is similar to the previous BASIC examples. There is an addition, however, in that line 60 is a PRINT statement that is part of the outer, or X%, loop. Prior to the X% loop recycling, the message in line 60 is displayed on the screen. The first two PRINT statements are associated with the nested, or Y%, loop. The last PRINT statement is associated with the outer, or X%, loop.

C Language:

```
main()
{



    int x, y;

    for (x = 0; x <= 100; ++x) {
        for (y = 100; y >= 0; --y) {
            printf("%d %d\n", x, y);
            printf("%d %d\n", x + 10, y + 10);
        }

        printf("CYCLING OUTER LOOP\n");
    }



}
```

Here, we seem to see braces all over the place; but it's fairly easy to see what is executed where by noting the position of the closing braces. We can tell that the first closing brace is associated with the *for* statement controlling the inner loop. The next closing brace is associated with the *for* statement controlling the outer loop. The final closing brace is associated with main(). This is a representation of two nested loops, each of which contains more than one associated statement. Two statements are associated with the outer or x loop. First, there is the inner *for* loop and then the final printf statement line, which prints the cycling prompt. The outer loop again views the *for* loop and its components as it would a single statement, It views the final printf statement line as the second statement associated with it. The inner, or y, loop sees the two printf statement lines that follow as its associations. Note that the x loop braces contain its entire contents. The y loop braces encompass this loop's entire contents. If we really wanted to get technical, it could be said that the x loop braces encompass the *for* statement line *and* the contents encompassed by the braces of the nested *for* statement line and the final printf statement line.

I'll admit that this can be quite complex at first. It may be easier for some readers to always include opening and closing braces with any *for* statement line, regardless of whether or not multiple statements associated with the loop are to follow. However, be warned that many tutorials on C will not use unnecessary braces.

BASIC Language:

```
10  X% = 0
20  WHILE X% <= 100
30  PRINT X%
40  X% = X% + 1
50  WEND
```

This program uses the BASIC WHILE-WEND statement to form a WHILE loop. The contents of the WHILE loop are executed until the test condition at the top of the loop (following WHILE) is no longer true. WEND signifies the end of the loop. When WEND is encountered, the loop recycles. This program will print the value of X% as long as X% is less than or equal to 100. In line 10, X% is assigned an initial value of 0. In BASIC, this is not necessary, since any variable that has not been preassigned is equal to 0 or "" in the case of a string variable. However, in C, it is absolutely necessary to make initial assignments to all variables. An unassigned numeric variable will not necessarily be equal to 0. As a matter of fact, it rarely will.

C Language:

```
main()
{

    int x;

    x = 0;

    while (x <= 100) {
        printf("%d\n", x);
        ++x;
    }

}
```

This program incorporates the *while* statement. The program is very similar to the BASIC version, although of course, there is no WEND statement. Here, *x* is declared int and is then assigned an initial value of 0. This assignment is mandatory in C language programs, whereas in BASIC, an unassigned numeric variable has a default value of 0. Note that an opening brace follows the *while* statement line. This is necessary because more than one statement will be executed within the *while* loop. This is usually the case with *while* loops, but there are some exceptions. As with the *for* loop, if only one statement is to be executed within the loop itself, the *while* loop statement need not be enclosed by braces.

Each time the loop cycles, the value of x is written to the screen by the printf line, and x is incremented by 1 (++x). At the beginning of each cycle, the value of x is tested to see if it is less than or equal to 100. If this occurs, the cycle is completed. If it is not the case, the loop is exited. The closing brace that falls beneath the *while* statement marks the loop termination point. Any statement lines that follow this closing brace are not part of the loop itself.

BASIC Language:

```
10  X% = 100
20  WHILE X%>= 0
30  PRINT X%
40  X% = X% – 1
50  WEND
```

This is the negative-stepping version of the previous BASIC program. The WHILE loop again prints the value of X%, which is assigned an initial value of 100. On each pass of the loop, X% is decremented by 1. When X% is less than 0 (-1), the loop terminates.

C Language:

```
main()
{

    int x;

    x = 100;

    while (x >= 0) {
        printf("%d\n", x);
        --x;
    }
```

This program is similar to the former C language version, except for the starting value of x, which is now 100. Also, x is decremented within the loop by the - -x notation. This program will display the value of x starting at 100 and ending at 0. When a value of -1 is detected, the loop test proves false. The loop is then exited and execution is terminated because no statements lie beyond the loop in this program.

BASIC Language:

```
10   X% = 0
20   Y% = 0
30   WHILE X% <= 10
40   WHILE Y% <= 5
50   PRINT X%;Y%
60   Y% = Y% + 1
70   WEND
80   X% = X% + 1
90   Y% = 0
100  WEND
```

This BASIC program demonstrates the use of a nested WHILE loop. The nested loop steps the value of Y% from 0 to 5. The PRINT statement and the Y% incrementing routine are associated only with the Y% loop. The first WEND statement terminates the Y% loop. At this point, X% is incremented by 1, and Y% is reassigned a value of 0. These last two lines are associated only with the outer, or X%, loop. When the program is run, the changing values of X% and Y% are displayed on the monitor screen.

C Language:

```
main()
{

    int x, y;

    x = y = 0;

    while (x <= 10) {
        while (y <= 5) {
            printf("%d %d\n", x, y);
            ++y;
        }

        ++x;
        y = 0;
    }

}
```

There's nothing highly unusual about the use of nested *while* loops in C. Just make certain you understand which braces surround statement lines associated with a particular loop. Variables *x* and *y* are declared ints. Both are assigned a value of 0 by the sequence x = y = 0. In most dialects of BASIC, this type of assignment is illegal; but in C, it's perfectly alright. This line is equivalent to:

```
x = 0;
y = 0;
```

The *while* loop that increments *y* is nested within the body of the *while* loop that increments *x*. The statements associated with the y loop are contained within braces, as are the statements associated with the x loop. In this example, the y loop in its entirety is looked upon as one statement by the x loop. The other two x loop statements are ++x; and y = 0;. The printf statement line and ++y; are the statements associated specifically with the y loop.

BASIC Language:

```
10   X% = 0
20   WHILE X% < = 10
30   FOR Y% = 0 To 5 STEP 1
40   PRINT X%;Y%
50   NEXT Y%
60   X% = X% + 1
70   WEND
```

This program nests a FOR-NEXT loop within the body of a WHILE-WEND loop. The WHILE loop will step X% from 0 to 10. On each pass of the WHILE loop, the for-next loop will count Y% from 0 to 5 and print the values of X% and Y% on the screen. When the for-next loop times out, X% is incremented by 1. When X% is incremented to 11, the WHILE test is no longer true, so the program terminates.

C Language:

```
main()
{

        int x, y;

        x = 0;
```

Program continues

```
while (x <= 10) {
        for (y = 0; y <= 5; ++y)
                printf("%d %d\n", x, y);

    ++x;
}


}
```

Nesting a *for* loop within the body of a *while* loop in C is quite simple; probably even simpler than doing the same thing in BASIC. Note in this example that no braces are required following the *for* loop, since only one statement line is to be executed. Braces do surround the *while* loop statements, which include the *for* loop and the x incrementer. Both x and y are declared ints, and x is assigned an initial value of 0. It is not necessary to assign y a value of 0 at this point in the program. This assignment is made immediately following the *for* statement, where the lower and upper values of y are assigned.

BASIC Language:

```
10   X% = 0
20   PRINT X%
30   X% = X% + 1
40   IF X% <= 20 THEN GOTO 20
```

This is an example of an exitable loop in BASIC. The value of X% is displayed on the screen, and X% is incremented by 1 as long as it is less than or equal to 20. If X% is more than 20, the program terminates. As mentioned previously, GOTO statements are often abused in BASIC. In other words, they are used when not absolutely necessary. Certainly, you've had the experience of trying to decipher a program that contained a large number of GOTO statements. The process can be quite tedious. This simple program example presents no problem; but remember that branch statements tend to hide the path of program flow. This is true in any language. Therefore, for program clarity, branch statements should be avoided where it is practical to do so.

C Language:

```
main()
{

    int x;

    x = 0;
```

Program continues

```
BR:
        printf("%d\n", x);
        ++x;

        if (x <= 20)
            goto BR;


    }
```

This is the exact C equivalent of the BASIC program, although it could be handled in a much simpler manner without the goto statement. However, goto is demonstrated here because there may come a time when its use is desirable. This will rarely occur—but it may.

In C, the goto statement must be followed by a label name. In this case, the label is "BR :". The colon that follows BR identifies it as a label. When a goto statement is encountered followed by the label name, a branch is made to the point in the program where the label was inserted. As in BASIC, branches may be made to a previous program line or to another point past the goto statement. With most C compilers, a label must begin with an alphabetic character. Numeric characters may follow. The *BR :* label preceding printf names the point in the program we wish to branch back to. When goto is encountered following the *if* statement line, it names the label to which the branch is to be made. Note here that the colon is not used, and the goto statement is terminated by the standard semicolon. This branch will continue to take place until the *if* test proves false (that is, *x* is more than 20). At this point, the program will terminate.

The following C language program demonstrates a better way of accomplishing the same operation without a goto statement. The program could have been written in practically the same way in BASIC for an improvement as well.

```
    main()
    {

        int x;

        x = 0;

        while (x <= 20) {
            printf("%d\n", x);
            ++x;
        }


    }
```

This program uses a *while* loop that executes a printf statement and increments *x*. When *x* is more than 20, execution terminates.

This is also a good point to introduce the *do-while* loop in C. This loop is not used very often, as it is very similar to the *while* loop. The *while* loop tests for a true-false condition at the top of the loop. The *do-while* loop tests for a true-false condition at the bottom of the loop. In the original BASIC and C language program examples, an *if* statement was used to test for a true-false condition at the bottom of the loop. The following C program uses *do-while* to effect a similar operation:

```
main()
{

    int x;

    x = 0;

    do {
        printf("%d\n", x);
        ++x;
    } while (x <= 20);


}
```

This program is exactly equivalent to the previous C language program as far as machine operation is concerned. Note that *do* is followed by an opening brace. This indicates that more than one statement is to be executed as a part of the loop. As with the other loops, if only one statement line is included in the body of the loop, braces are not necessary. The *do-while* loop more or less says, "do the following," (enclosed in braces). The while portion says, "go back to *do* while the test line is true." Note that a semicolon follows the *while* test line. This is necessary because *while* is treated as a statement. Notice also that the closing brace for the *do* loop statements precedes the use of *while*. One may think of *while* in this example as an *if* statement followed by a goto. It says while *x* is less than or equal to 20, goto *do*.

Again, *do-while* statements are used very rarely; but there are certain cases where it is advantageous to test for a true-false condition at the bottom of the loop rather than at the top. In these cases, *do-while* can be quite effective.

BASIC Language:

```
10  FOR X% = 0 TO 100 STEP 1
20  PRINT X%
30  IF X% = 20 THEN GOTO 50
40  NEXT X%
50  PRINT "LOOP EXITED"
```

This is a nonsense program, in that a loop is set up to count from 0 to 100; but an IF-THEN statement is included to exit the loop when X% equals 20. However, it makes an ideal example of a conditional loop exit that can be converted to a C language demonstration program.

C Language:

```
main()
{

    int x;

    for (x = 0; x <= 100; ++x) {
        printf("%d\n", x);

        if (x == 20)
            goto BR;
    }
BR:
    printf("LOOP EXITED\n");

}
```

The C language version closely copies the program in BASIC. Each time the loop cycles, if tests for a condition of *x* being equal to 20. When this occurs, the goto statement is executed and branches to label *BR :*. Here, the printf line displays the closing message on the screen.

Again, a goto has been used, and in C, such statements are almost never necessary. In this example, a goto was used to break out of the loop and branch to the first statement immediately following the loop. In C, there's another statement that can take the place of goto in this particular example. The *break* statement is used to exit a loop prematurely. The following program is the equivalent of the program just presented, but uses *break* instead of goto.

```
main()
{

    int x;

    for (x = 0; x <= 100; ++x) {
        printf("%d\n", x);

        if (x == 20)
            break;
    }

    printf("LOOP EXITED\n");

}
```

We have no control over where *break* branches to. Its sole purpose is to exit a loop. Execution resumes at the first statement immediately following the loop. We can say, then, that *break* brings about early termination of a loop. In this example, it has been used to take the place of goto, since all this latter statement did was branch out of the loop to the first executable line following the loop. Again, it is more efficient to avoid the use of goto.

BASIC Language:

```
10  INPUT X%
20  IF X% = 20 THEN PRINT X% ELSE PRINT X%*X%
```

This program demonstrates the use of IF-THEN-ELSE. If X% is equal to 20, its value will be printed to the screen. If it is not equal to 20, ELSE takes over, and X% times X% is printed.

C Language:

```
main()
{

    int x;

    scanf("%d", &x);

    if (x == 20)
        printf("%d\n", x);
    else
        printf("%d\n", x * x);

}
```

The *if-else* sequence in C is quite easy to use. Note that a single statement is executed if the *if* test proves true. Therefore, no braces are needed. Also, a single statement is executed when *else* takes over, so no braces are needed with the *else* portion of this program. The first printf line is executed when *x* is equal to 20. If it is not equal to 20, the second printf line is executed.

BASIC Language:

```
10  INPUT X%
20  IF X% = 20 THEN PRINT X% ELSE IF X% = 10 THEN PRINT X% – 1
    ELSE PRINT X%*X%
```

This program makes use of IF-THEN-ELSE and ELSE-IF. If X% is equal to 20, this value will be displayed on the screen. If X% is equal to 10, this value minus 1 will be displayed on the screen. If neither of these conditions is true, the value of X% times X% will be displayed.

C Language:

```
main()
{

        int x;

        scanf("%d", &x);

        if (x == 20)
                printf("%d\n", x);
        else if (x == 10)
                printf("%d\n", x - 1);
        else
                printf("%d\n", x * x);

}
```

The C language version follows the same route as the BASIC program, although it's a little easier to understand because multiple lines are used to express what was expressed in a single line in the BASIC program. From looking at the C program, we can see that the value of *x* is displayed when *x* is equal to 20. However, if *x* is equal to 10, *x* minus 1 is displayed. If neither of these conditions is true, *x* times *x* is displayed. If multiple statements were to be carried out in association with *if*, a brace would follow the *if* statement line (opening). A closing brace would mark termination of the statements to be carried out under *if*. The same applies to *else-if* and *else*. Remember, *else-if* and *else* are not considered statements associated with *if*, and therefore are not included within the braces.

SUMMARY

Several of the statements found in C have been discussed in this chapter. These are the ones most pertinent to BASIC. The remaining C language statements will be discussed in later chapters. It should be clear that the statements common to C bear a direct relationship to those equivalent statements in BASIC. It shouldn't take long for persons making the switch from BASIC to C to obtain a good understanding of these statements. To reiterate, while goto is a valid statement in C, it should be used conservatively. I think you will find that the *while* loop in C can be used to effectively avoid the use of goto in most instances. Goto statements tend to hide program flow, making the source program quite difficult to decipher, especially if it is long and complex.

ASSIGNMENTS

1. Write a program in C using the for statement to count from -10 to +10, printing the count value to the screen in horizontal format.
2. Write the same program using the while statement.
3. Modify the last program to print the message "COUNT = 0" when the counting variable is indeed equal to 0.
4. Write a program using two while statements. The outer loop should count from 0 to 20. The inner loop should count from 20 to 0.
5. Write a program using two for statements that does the same thing as the previous program.

5

STRING MANIPULATION IN C

C language is extremely useful in handling character strings. In previous chapters, we have used char arrays and char pointers (char *) to act as string variables. In most cases, C treats these two types identically.

In this chapter, we will deal extensively with C language string utility functions such as strlen, which is the equivalent of LEN in BASIC; strcmp, which compares one string with another; strcpy, which copies the contents of one string into another; and several others.

BASIC Language:

```
10  A$ = "COMPUTER"
20  X% = LEN(A$)
30  PRINT X%
```

This program assigns A$ the value "COMPUTER." In line 20, X% is assigned the value of the length of A$ in characters by using the LEN function. Since there are eight letters in "COMPUTER," X% will now be equal to 8. This value is displayed on the screen by the PRINT statement in line 30.

C Language:

```
main()
{

        int x;
        char *a;

        a = "COMPUTER";

        x = strlen(a);

        printf("%d\n", x);

}
```

In C, the *strlen* function is the equivalent of the LEN function in BASIC. In this program, x is declared an int, while a is declared a string pointer. Variable a is assigned the value of "COMPUTER" and strlen then returns the number of characters in a to integer x. The last line prints this value on the screen. As is the case with most of the string functions in C, the variable may be declared a string pointer or a character array. For example, the program could have been written as:

```
int x;
char a[] = {'C', 'O', 'M', 'P', 'U', 'T', 'E', 'R', '\0'};
x = strlen(a);
```

This is one way of assigning a string value to a character array. Note that no size designation was included between the brackets that signify an array in the char a declaration. When char [ ] is followed by an equal sign along with the values to be placed in the array, the assignment of the proper number of array positions is handled automatically. Notice that the last character placed in the array is a backslash-zero. This is the null character and is automatically placed at the end of character strings by the compiler in order to signify the end of a particular string. In this type of assignment, however, it is necessary to include the null character as a part of the array. Instead of the above modification, we could also have used gets to place a string from the keyboard into array a. In this case, the null terminator would automatically be inserted by the compiler.

BASIC Language:

```
10  A$ = "COMPU"
20  B$ = "TER"
```

```
30  A$ = A$ + B$
40  PRINT A$
```

In BASIC, we can add one string value to the end of another. This is exactly what is done in this program. A$ is first assigned a portion of the word "COMPUTER." B$ is then assigned the remaining portion. In line 30, A$ is reassigned its own value plus the value of B$. After line 30, A$ is equal to "COMPU" plus "TER," or "COMPUTER." The value of A$ is displayed by the PRINT statement in line 40.

C Language:

```
main()
{

    char *a, *b;

    a = "COMPU";
    b = "TER";

    strcat(a, b);

    printf("%s\n", a);

}
```

In C, the *strcat* function can take the place of the plus sign in BASIC when string values are to be added. Technically, the values are not really added in BASIC. In this example, the contents of B$ were catenated to the value of A$. In this terminology, catenated can be defined as "tacked on." The line strcat(a, b); catenates the contents of *b* to the end of *a*. Technically, *a* and *b* both contain their assigned characters plus the backslash-zero null terminators. Strcat uses the null terminator at the end of *a* to act as the starting point for catenation of the first character in *b*. When the process is complete, *a* is equal to the word "COMPUTER" plus the null terminator at its end.

Since all this program does (operationally) is print the catenated values of A$ and B$ in BASIC or *a* and *b* in C, we could have eliminated the A$ + B$ and strcat(a, b); lines and simply gone with:

```
40  PRINT A$ + B$
```

and

```
printf("%s%s\n", a, b);
```

However, the purpose of these examples is to show how the contents of a string variable may be altered by catenating another string variable.

BASIC Language:

```
10  A$ = "ONE"
20  FOR X = 1 TO 3 STEP 1
30  INPUT B$
40  A$ = A$ + B$
50  NEXT X
60  PRINT A$
```

This program makes an initial assignment to A$ of "ONE." A for-next loop is then entered, which cycles three times. On each cycle of the loop, the INPUT statement requests input via the keyboard. Line 40 adds the keyboard input to the end of A$ on each pass. When the loop is exited, the total value of A$ is displayed. Assuming a loop input of "TWO," "THREE," and "FOUR," the final value of A$ would be "ONETWOTHREEFOUR."

C Language:

```
main()
{

        int x;
        char *a, *b;

        a = "ONE";

        for (x = 1; x <= 3; ++x) {
                gets(b);
                strcat(a, b);
        }

        printf("%s\n", a);

}
```

In this program, *x* is declared an int, while *a* and *b* are declared character string pointers. Variable *a* is initially assigned a value of "ONE." When the *for* loop is entered, gets is used to retrieve the value of *b* from the keyboard.

The strcat function catenates the contents of *b* to *a*. This occurs each time the loop cycles. Upon exiting the loop, printf displays the total value of *a* on the screen.

BASIC Language:

```
10  B$ = "COMPUTER"
20 A$ = B$
30  PRINT A$
```

This program simply copies the contents of one string to another and then displays the contents of the copied string on the screen. Initially, string variable B$ is assigned the value of "COMPUTER." Line 20 then assigns A$ the value of B$. Line 30 displays the value of A$.

C Language:

```
main()
{

    char *a, *b;

    b = "COMPUTER";
    a = b;

    printf("%s\n", a);

}
```

The C language version mimics the BASIC program in almost every way. As long as we're dealing with two char * variables, this mimicry will work quite well. However, one must remember that character arrays may also be used in place of character string variables, and here, some difficulty is encountered, at least when using the format shown here.

The following program assigns variable *a* as a 65-element character array. Variable *b* is a character string pointer. The assignment to *b* is appropriate. However, since we are dealing with two types of variables (character array and character pointer), we cannot use the a = b assignment. This program is incorrect and will not run.

WRONG:

```
main()
{

        char a[65], *b;

        b = "COMPUTER";
        a = b;

        printf("%s\n", a);

}
```

The following program demonstrates the correct way to copy the value in character pointer b to character array a.

```
main()
{

        char a[65], *b;

        b = "COMPUTER";
        strcpy(a, b);

        printf("%s\n", a);

}
```

This program uses the *strcpy* function, which copies one string value contained in a variable to another variable. It makes no difference what types of variables are used as long as each is capable of holding the string value. Using strcpy, we can copy the contents of one character array into another character array, the contents of a character array into a string pointer, the contents of a string pointer into a character array, or the contents of a string pointer to another string pointer. In BASIC, string variables are used to hold string values. In C, however, string values may be contained in a character pointer variable or a character array. To illustrate the equivalents of character pointers and character arrays, examine the following BASIC program:

WRONG:

```
10  DIM B(3)
20  B(0) = 68
30  B(1) = 73
40  B(2) = 83
50  B(3) = 75
60  A$ = B
```

This program obviously will not work, since we cannot assign the entire contents of array B to A$ with the assignment line shown in line 60 of this program. This is not an exact equivalent of the incorrect C program, but it's about as close as we can come in BASIC. In C, character values are assigned as integers. The numbers assigned to each element in array B represent the ASCII codes of the letters we wish to represent. This sequence of numbers represents the word "DISK." Line 60 is representative here of the assignment the incorrect C language program attempted to make.

However, by using the strcpy function, we overcome any problems that may be encountered in assigning any character array or string pointer the value of another type of variable. Again, strcpy can only use variable types that are adequate to hold the desired string. The strcpy function is used in a format of:

```
strcpy(to, from);
```

The contents of "from" are copied to "to." One should remember that C treats assigned character arrays and assigned character pointers almost identically, in that either may be used to contain character strings. In most instances, these two types of variables may be used interchangeably. However, it is always best to use strcpy when assigning the contents of one variable to another. This function must be used only when copying string values and not for numeric values.

BASIC Language:

```
10  B$ = "COMPUTER"
20  INPUT A$
30  IF A$ = B$ THEN PRINT "The strings are identical.": END
40  PRINT "The strings do not match."
```

Initially, this program assigns B$ the value of "COMPUTER." The INPUT statement is then used to accept input from the keyboard. Line 30 tests to see if the keyboard input is the same as B$. If so, a message is printed indicating that the two are identical, and the program is terminated. If the two strings are not identical, line 40 is executed, which prints a prompt indicating that the two strings do not match.

The following C program is not correct but illustrates a typical attempt by persons new to C to mimic the above BASIC program.

WRONG:

```
main()
{

    char *a, *b;

    b = "COMPUTER";

    gets(a);

    if (a == b) {
        printf("The strings are identical.\n");
        exit(0);
    }

    printf("The strings do not match.\n");

}
```

The program is perfectly all right until we come to the comparison made in the *if* statement line. Due to the way strings are stored in C, we cannot test for identical values using a==b. This program will work perfectly if a way can be found to make the needed comparison between the contents of *a* and *b*. The reason a==b is not valid is due to the way C stores the contents of string variables. In order to make a true comparison, it is necessary to compare each element contained in *a* with each element contained in *b*. Fortunately, there is a standard function in C that is used to make comparisons of string variables. This is called *strcmp* and stands for "string compare." This function compares the contents of two string variables and returns 0 if the two are identical. If the two are not identical, the return value will be less than or more than 0. The following program shows the correct method of mimicing the BASIC program:

C Language:

```
main()
{

    char *a, *b;

    b = "COMPUTER";

    gets(a);

    if (strcmp(a, b) == 0) {
        printf("The strings are identical.\n");
        exit(0);
    }

    printf("The strings do not match.\n");

}
```

Notice that the program is identical to the previous incorrect one, with the exception that the strcmp function is included as part of the *if* statement line. The format for strcmp is:

$$x = strcmp(a, b);$$

where x is declared an int and a and b are character arrays or character pointers or a combination of both. Yes, strcmp will compare the contents of a character array to a contents of a character pointer. This is necessary in C because either type of variable can be used to contain a string. If the contents of a and b are identical, a value of 0 will be returned to x.

In the program example, the equivalent of integer variable x was never used. Its use is not necessary in this example, since strcmp(a, b) will be equal to 0 if the strings are identical or more or less than 0 if they are not. In this line, we are comparing the value of strcmp with 0 to see if the two are identical. This line could also have been written as:

$$if ((x = strcmp(a, b)) == 0)$$

This assumes that x was previously declared an int value. However, this means that more typing is required to input the program line. For the sake of efficiency, the abbreviation used in the example program is preferred.

This substitution line really says:

```
x = strcmp(a, b);
if (x == 0)
```

By using the format shown in the program, we shorten overall program input time.

BASIC Language:

```
10  INPUT A$
20  IF A$ = "COMPUTER" THEN PRINT "That is the word I was looking for.": END
30  PRINT "That's not the word."
```

This program uses only a single string variable. Line 20 tests for the input of the word "COMPUTER." If this word is input, a prompt is displayed, and the program is terminated. If not, line 30 is executed, indicating another word was input.

C Language:

```
main()
{

    char *a;

    gets(a);

    if (strcmp(a, "COMPUTER") == 0) {
        printf("That is the word I was looking for.\n")
        exit(0);
    }

    printf("That's not the word.\n");

}
```

In this example, strcmp is again used, but this time to compare the contents of a character pointer variable with an actual value rather than the value contained in another variable. The *if* statement line compares the contents of *a* with the string constant "COMPUTER." This duplicates exactly what was done in the BASIC program. Many beginning C programmers are under the false impression that any function that calls for a string pointer cannot use a string constant. This is not true. In almost every instance, string variable types may be replaced with string constants, as long as the constants are contained within quotation marks. This also applies to strlen, strcat, and all others.

BASIC Language:

```
10 INPUT A$
20 WHILE A$ <> "END"
30 PRINT A$
40 INPUT A$
50 WEND
```

This program first accepts an input that is assigned to A$. A *while* loop is entered and continues to cycle as long as A$ is not equal to "END." The first INPUT statement in line 10 is executed only once. This gives us an initial value of A$, which is tested by the *while* loop. As long as A$ is not equal to "END," lines 30 and 40 are executed. Line 30 displays the value of A$, and line 40 allows another value of A$ to be input. When A$ is equal to "END," the program terminates.

C Language:

```
main ()
{

    char *a;

    while ((strcmp (gets (a), "END")) != 0)
        puts (a);

}
```

The C language version is quite simple and takes less time to input. This program is an excellent demonstration of C language shorthand and the strcmp function. Here, gets(a), which is equivalent to INPUT A$ in BASIC, and strcmp are included within a single line. This program is equivalent to the longer:

```
gets(a);
while (strcmp(a, "END") != 0) {
    puts (a);
    gets (a);
}
```

This modification more closely mimics the BASIC program in style; but the original C language program is far more efficient, at least from the stand-point of programming time. Here, gets(a) is used as one of the arguments for strcmp, while "END" is the other argument. The value returned from the keyboard to gets is compared with string constant "END." If they are identical, a value of 0 is returned. The *while* loop cycles as long as a 0 is not returned.

It should be noted again that the string functions will work equally well with character pointers, character arrays, or constant values. Many will even work with other functions that return string values, as in the above example where gets is used as an argument for strcmp.

BASIC Language:

```
10  DIM A$(5)
20  FOR X = 0 TO 5
30  INPUT A$(X)
40  NEXT X
50  FOR X = 0 TO 5
60  PRINT A$(X)
70  NEXT X
80  END
```

This program initializes an array to hold six elements. This is a string array, so each element will be a string value. Line 20 begins a for-next loop that counts from 0 to 5. Each time the loop cycles, an INPUT statement is executed. The keyboard input is assigned to the string array element that matches the value of X. When the loop is exited, another loop is begun that prints the contents of each element in the array sequentially. The program then terminates.

C Language:

```c
main()
{

    int x;
    char *a[5];

    for (x = 0; x <= 5; ++x)
        gets(a[x]);

    for (x = 0; x <= 5; ++x)
        printf("%s\n", a[x]);

    exit(0);

}
```

In C, the equivalent of the BASIC language string array is an array of pointers. Each element in a pointer array points to the memory location where the string is stored. In this example, the array is initialized with the char *a[5]; declaration. This indicates that a pointer array is to be established that will hold a total of six string pointers (0-5 equals 6). As in the BASIC program, two for-next loops are set up. The first one uses gets to receive the information from the keyboard. This information is assigned to a[x] on each pass of the loop. In the second loop, the printf statement is used to print the string pointed to by a[x]. In BASIC, we seem to assume that each element of the array holds the entire contents of the string. This is not a correct assumption. Indeed, each element contains the equivalent of a pointer to the string just as it does in C. Remember, a pointer is a value that gives the memory address of the value sought. If a string array in BASIC really held the string value, it would have to be initialized to hold the number of characters in the string total. Remember, in C, string pointers are variables and may generally be handled as though they contained the actual string values. From an operational standpoint, this would seem to be the case.

ASSIGNMENTS

1. Write a program that accepts input from the keyboard, commits it to a string variable, and displays each input on the screen.
2. Write a program that accepts and displays keyboard string input until the word "END" is input.
3. Write a program using a character pointer array that accepts five keyboard inputs and displays the input in horizontal format.

6 C LANGUAGE FUNCTIONS

Throughout this book, I have made constant reference to program functions. A function may be thought of as a kind of subroutine or mini-program that performs a specific operation. The function may operate on its own without any argument, or it may operate on values that are passed to it as arguments. Every program written in C thus far in this book could also be committed to the category of function with very little modification. The following examples in BASIC will better describe exactly what a function is and how it works. However, one should always be aware of the fact that in C, a function is simply a complete program that's written like any other program. A true C language program, however, is made up of one or more functions. Therefore, C language programs are simply collections of smaller C language programs called functions which perform specific operations.

The following BASIC program prints various words to the screen. Between each print sequence is a time delay loop that creates a pause between the end of one print sequence and the beginning of another.

```
10 PRINT "HELLO"
20 FOR X=1 TO 1000:NEXT X
30 PRINT "GOODBYE"
40 FOR X=1 TO 1000:NEXT X
50 PRINT "GREETINGS"
60 FOR X=1 TO 1000:NEXT X
70 PRINT "SO LONG"
80 END
```

Obviously, this program is far more complex than it needs to be. Note that lines 20, 40, and 60 are identical. These are the time delay loops that create the pause between each print sequence. This program is written more efficiently as:

```
 10  PRINT "HELLO"
 20  GOSUB 90
 30  PRINT "GOODBYE"
 40  GOSUB 90
 50  PRINT "GREETINGS"
 60  GOSUB 90
 70  PRINT "SO LONG"
 80  END
 90  FOR X=1 TO 1000:NEXT X
100  RETURN
```

We still have the same number of lines. However, each time a delay loop is needed, GOSUB is used to access the subroutine in lines 90 and 100. Each time GOSUB is encountered, there is a branch to line 90. The RETURN statement in line 100 branches back to the line following the one that caused the initial branch to the subroutine.

In C, we can think of functions as subroutines that are called by name rather than by a branch-line number. An appropriate name for a function that brings about a time delay is "pause."

BASIC Language:

```
10  REM PAUSE
20  FOR X=1 TO 1000:NEXT X
30  RETURN
```

This example illustrates a subroutine that creates a pause while the computer counts from 1 to 1000. This is not a full program but only a subroutine used as an example to illustrate a C language function equivalent.

C Language:

```
pause()
{

        int x;

        for (x = 1; x <= 1000; ++x)
                ;

}
```

This is not a complete C language program but a function whose name is "pause." Here, the name is very important, because this function may be called from a C language program by its name. Looking at the body of the function itself, we can see that it follows standard C language format. Variable x is declared an int, and is then stepped from 1 to 1000 in a *for* loop. This loop has no argument, but a semicolon must be included to indicate the null argument. This function will bring about a pause equal to the time it takes the computer to step x from 1 to 1000.

Note that the beginning of the function uses its name rather than main( ). The two parens following "pause" contain no argument designation. This indicates that the function requires no argument and is self-operating. The following C language program shows how the pause function is used to exactly duplicate the previous BASIC language program which printed information to the screen with a delay after each screen write, accessed by GOSUBs.

```
...
main()
{

        printf("%s\n", "HELLO");
        pause();

        printf("%s\n", "GOODBYE");
        pause();

        printf("%s\n", "GREETINGS");
        pause();

        printf("%s\n", "SO LONG");

        exit(O);

}
pause()
{

        int x;

        for (x = 1; x <= 1000; ++x)
                ;

}
```

Note that this program begins with main( ), as do all C language programs. String constants are used with each printf line to display the various words on the screen. After each printf statement line, the pause function is called by name. In BASIC terminology, each time the pause function is encountered in the C language program, there is a GOSUB to pause( ) at the bottom of the program. The pause function is executed, and control returns to the line following the call to pause. The pause function is not a part of the main body of the C language program. The closing brace to the main body of the C language program can be seen just above the name of the pause function. Therefore, the pause function lies outside the body of the C language program and is called from C. It is by this same method that the standard functions in C have been written. Functions like gets, printf, and so on are called as functions from main( ). This means that in C, any handy little program you write can be built into the function format and called as any other C language function.

One must remember that functions are separate from the main body of the program and cannot use any values contained in the main program unless they are passed to the function as arguments. In the pause function, you will see that x has been declared an int value. This variable, however, is common only to the pause function itself. We could also have declared x an int value in the main body of the program. However, this variable would have been treated independently. It would bear no relationship whatsoever to the value of x in the pause function proper. A function can only use a main program value or variable when it has been passed to the function as an argument.

BASIC Language:

```
10  X = 10
20  GOSUB 100
30  PRINT Y
40  END
100 Y = 2*X
110 RETURN
```

This BASIC program assigns X a value of 10. The subroutine beginning at line 100 assigns Y a value of 2 times X. Line 30 then prints the value of Y to the screen.

C Language:

```
main()
{

    int x, y;

    x = 10;
    y = mult(x);
```

Program continues

```
        printf("%d\n", y);

}
mult(a)
int a;
{

        return(2 * a);

}
```

In C, unlike BASIC, the function has no way of knowing the value of any variable within the main program unless it is passed as a part of the function call. In this example, the subroutine that multiplies x times 2 is presented as a function named "mult." Since the main purpose of this function is to multiply a value within the main body of the program by 2, the value must be passed to it. The line y = mult(x); tells us that integer y is equal to whatever value is returned by the mult function. The argument to the mult function (the value passed) is the value of x in the main program. In the function itself, note that the variable argument is identified by the letter a. This is done simply to show you that this argument need not be the same as the argument variable used when it was called. We could also have used mult(x), mult(z), or any other legal variable name in the mult function proper. Remember, the variables used by a function are treated independently of those used within the main body of the program.

However, any arguments that are passed to a function must be declared within the function itself. Since the passed value represented by x was previously declared an integer within the main program, it must be declared an integer within the function; thus, the int a; declaration. There is an opening brace in the function that indicates the start of execution of the main body of the function program. This program contains only the return statement and is followed by a closing brace which indicates that the function is terminated. Control then returns to the main program.

In C functions, the return statement simply indicates what value is to be returned to the main body of the program. The argument for return is $2 * a$, which means that a value equal to 2 times the past value of a is to be returned. This means that mult(x) in the main program is replaced by the value of 2 times x. Remember, variable a in the function represents the same value as variable x in the main program. The printf line in the main program then displays the value of y, which is 20.

Any variables that are declared within a function prior to the opening brace are the passed variables from the main program. Any variables declared after the opening brace are variables that are internal to the function itself. These variables are used only by the function and may bear the same names as those within the main program, although the two are separate and independent.

BASIC Language:

```
10  A$ = "HELLO"
20  GOSUB 100
30  PRINT A$
40  END
100 A$ = A$ + "GOODBYE"
110 RETURN
```

In this program, A$ is assigned an initial value of "HELLO." When the subroutine is accessed, A$ is reassigned the value of itself plus "GOODBYE." When line 30 is executed, the string "HELLOGOODBYE" will be displayed.

C Language:

```
main()
{

    char *a;

    a = "HELLO";
    change(a);
    printf("%s\n", a);

}
change(c)
char *c;
{

    strcat(c, "GOODBYE");

}
```

In this example, the BASIC subroutine has been replaced with a C language function named "change." The only argument to change is the passed value of *a*. We have used a variable named "*c*" in the function itself, but again, the variable designator here is of no consequence. Note that c is declared a char * value before the main body of the function is entered. The strcat function (standard in C) is used to copy the string constant "GOOD-BYE" to the end of c. This value is passed back to the original call to change. Therefore, a is now equal to "HELLOGOODBYE." It is not necessary to use the return statement here, since control will return to the main program after the termination brace in the function. Note that this function operated on the past value itself rather than returning a value based upon the passed value. This function changes the value of a in the main body of the program, as evidenced by the screen write when printf is executed. When functions must change the value that is passed to them, the values that are passed must be pointers. A string array value is a pointer, as is the character pointer value in this example. This is important to remember when dealing with numbers such as ints, floats, and doubles. If you pass a value of a number to a function, the function cannot change the value of this number. This can be done only when a numeric value is passed as a pointer or by memory location. This was not the case with the mult function, which passed a value. The function itself simply used the value to come up with a return value. It did not alter the value of the passed variable itself.

The following program shows a common mistake beginning C programmers make:

```
main()
{

        int a;

        a = 10;
        change(a);
        printf("%d\n", a);

}
change(c)                                      /*WRONG*/
int c;
{

        c = c * 2;

}
```

This is a modification of the original change function intended to change the value of the integer passed to it. This won't work because the pass was made by value rather than by memory location; and a C function cannot change any variable whose value is not passed by memory location. This function will work, however, by calling change(&*a*). When this is done in the main body of the program, the location of *a* is passed, and the change will indeed be passed back to the main program.

BASIC Language:

```
10  X% = 3
20  Y% = 10
30  SWAP X%, Y%
40  PRINT X%; Y%
```

This program uses the SWAP statement in Microsoft BASIC to exchange the values of two variables. Initially, X% is equal to 3, and Y% is equal to 10; but after the SWAP statement is executed, X% will be equal to 10, and Y% will be equal to 3. Line 40 simply displays the exchanged values on the screen. Problem: The standard C language function set contains no swap function. Answer: Write one of your own.

Let's figure out how to write a swap function. First, we'll do it in BASIC as a subroutine, since BASIC is the language you're most familiar with at this time.

```
10   X% = 3
20   Y% = 10
30   GOSUB 100
40   PRINT X%; Y%
50   END
100  REM SWAP FUNCTION
110  Z% = X%
120  X% = Y%
130  Y% = Z%
140  RETURN
```

Lines 100 through 140 represent a function or subroutine in BASIC that corresponds with the SWAP statement. All we need is a third variable to temporarily hold the value of one of the passed variables. Here, Z% is temporarily assigned the value of X%. Then X% is reassigned the value of Y%. Finally, Y% is reassigned the value of Z%. The end result is that X% is now equal to the original value of Y%, and Y% is equal to the original value of X%.

C Language:

```
main()
{

      int x, y;

      x = 3;
      y = 10;

      swap(&x, &y);

      printf("%d %d\n", x, y);

}
swap(a, b)
int *a, *b;
{

      int c;

      c = *a;
      *a = *b;
      *b = c;

}
```

Here is the swap function written in C along with a program that matches the BASIC version. Note that swap is called in the main program with passed arguments that are preceded by ampersands. This means that the arguments to swap are passed by memory location. This is mandatory because the function is to change the actual values passed to it.

In the function itself, a and b are declared integer pointers. They are pointers because an asterisk precedes each variable name. This means that a and b, which were passed by x and y in the main function call, are declared integer pointers, or pointers to the values those variables contain. Within the executable body of the function, our temporary storage variable is declared an int. It is not necessary to declare this an integer pointer because this variable is exclusive to the function. Following this, c is assigned the value of integer pointer a. Integer pointer a is assigned the value of integer pointer b. Finally, integer pointer b is assigned the value of int c. These rearrangements are passed back to the main program as integer pointers. Therefore, the actual values of the variables in the main program have been altered. Remember, you cannot pass arguments to a function by value when it is desirable to change the value of a variable within the main program. Such values must be passed by location.

BASIC Language:

```
10  X = 1.219
20  GOSUB 100
30  PRINT Y
40  END
100  Y = X*2
110  RETURN
```

This program is very similar to an earlier one in which we used the mult function to arrive at a C language version. However, the previous program used the mult function to act upon an integer value and return an integer value. In C, all functions that return numeric values will return integers by default unless special declarations are made. If a function is to return other than an int value (numeric functions only), the type of value it is to return must be declared at the beginning of the main program and in the function name itself.

C Language:

```
main()
{

     float x, y, multf();

     x = 1.219;
     y = multf(x);

     printf("%f\n", y);

}
float multf(a)
float a;
{

     return(a * 2);

}
```

In this example, the function that multiplies floating-point value x by 2 must return a floating-point value. Therefore, the function (named multf) is declared a float in the main program, and its name is preceded by the word "float" in the function itself. This is a signal to the computer that a floating-point value is to be returned rather than the default integer value. Notice in the first declaration (within the main program) that multf is followed by two parens. This simply indicates that multf is a function, not a float variable. The rest of the program is identical to the previous version. However, the inclusion of float in declaring and naming the function means that a float value will be returned. Incidentally, float functions are rarely used in C. Most functions that do not return integers will be declared doubles to take advantage of the higher precision. A good example is the standard C language function atof, which returns a double-precision value. Both float and double name variables that will hold floating-point numbers. A double, however, has a much higher precision.

Personalized C language functions are one of the greatest attributes of this language. With enough experience, a large library of personalized functions may be written to shorten programming time. For example, if you use a large number of alphabetizing subroutines in writing programs, the subroutine can be written once and used in many different programs. Such a function might be named "alpha" and would include, as arguments, a character pointer array to hold the returned, sorted values and an integer to name the number of elements to be alphabetized. In C, qsort is well-known as such a function. While not specifically a part of C, it is usually a part of UNIX, in which C is resident.

While not specifically functions, macros are often used in C to perform many of the same operations or to replace functions. A macro or macro substitution is written in much the same manner as a DEF FN substitution in BASIC.

BASIC Language:

```
10  DEF FNSQUARE(X) = X*X
20  A = 10
30  B = FNSQUARE(A)
40  PRINT B
```

This program uses the DEF FN statement to define a function. The function is named FNSQUARE and is equal to its argument times its argument. In line 20, A is assigned a value of 10. In line 30, B is equal to FNSQUARE(A). The square of A, which is 10, is 100. Therefore, B is equal to 100.

C Language:

```
#define  square(X)  X * X
main()
{

    int a, b;

    a = 10;
    b = square(a);

    printf("%d\n", b);

}
```

This C language version uses a macro substitution rather than a separate function named "square." The macro substitution is named "square," but it operates in a completely different manner than a function. Instead of DEF FN, a macro substitution is named using the #define preprocessor directive. All #define does is tell the processor during the compilation of the main program to replace square(argument) with argument * argument. This will occur anytime square(argument) is used within the program. During compilation, when the processor receives the line:

```
b = square(a);
```

it is replaced with:

```
b = a * a;
```

Macros are quite valuable, in that they are quick to write and aren't very particular about argument types. This is because macros are not passed arguments as functions are. They simply substitute one line for another. The function equivalent of the above C language program is:

```
main()
{

    int a, b;

    a = 10;
    b = square(a);

    printf("%d\n", b);

}
```

Program continues

```
square(x)
int x;
{

    return(x * x);

}
```

Here, square is written as a function that is passed a value. In this case, the value is named an integer (within the function), and by default, an integer value will be returned. But what if you want a function that can be passed and will return an integer, a float, or even a character string? The answer is that you either have to do this through macro substitution or write three different functions with three different names that will address the three types of data to be passed and returned. The square function shown above can only receive and return integer values. However, the macro version of square can be used with any type of numeric variable. The original program using the macro could be modified to declare a and b as float values. The macro substitution would still be fine, since:

b = square(a);

is replaced by:

b = a * a;

Since b and a have previously been declared (floats in this modification), there is no problem. Macros are often used in place of functions where many different types of values must be passed.

BASIC Language:

```
10 X% = 3
20 Y% = 10
30 A$ = "HELLO"
40 B$ = "GOODBYE"
50 I = 1.219
60 J = 4.6275
70 SWAP X%,Y%
80 SWAP A$,B$
90 SWAP I,J
100 PRINT X%;Y%;A$;B$;I;J
```

This program uses three types of variables in BASIC. X% and Y% are integer variables, while A$ and B$ are string variables. Finally, I and J are floating-point variables. Even though we're dealing with three different types of variables, the SWAP statement in BASIC can be used with any of them, as evidenced by the SWAP statements used in lines 70 through 90. Line 100 displays the swapped values of all variables in the program.

C Language:

```
#define   swap(A, B, C)      C = A; A = B; B = C;
main()
{

     int x, y, xy;
     char *a, *b, *ab;
     float i, j, ij;

     x = 3;
     y = 10;
     a = "HELLO";
     b = "GOODBYE";
     i = 1.219;
     j = 4.6275;

     swap(x, y, xy);
     swap(a, b, ab);
     swap(i, j, ij);

     printf("%d %d %s %s %f %f\n", x, y, a, b, i, j);

}
```

This program uses one swap macro substitution to closely emulate the use of the SWAP statement in BASIC. Here, swap is #defined as containing three arguments. This may seem strange at first, since we only wish to swap the values of two variables. You will remember, however, in the previous discussion of the swap function, that it was necessary to come up with a temporary storage variable in order to make the swap. The swap is made in the same way within the macro, with C being temporarily assigned the value of A, A the value of B, and, finally, B the value of C. When defining macros, we often use upper-case variable names, although lower-case letters may be used as well.

Within the C program, an extra variable type is declared for each of the variables whose values are to be swapped. These extra variables are *xy*, *ab*, and *ij*. These are also known as dummy variables. They are declared simply to temporarily hold values during the swapping process. The following six lines assign values to each of the variables. The next three lines use swap to swap the values of the first two variable arguments. The third variable argument in each swap line is the dummy variable, which temporarily holds the value of the first variable during the swapping process. For instance, the first swap line is:

swap(x, y, xy);

and is substituted with:

xy = x; x = y; y = xy;

This notation is equivalent to a multiple statement line in BASIC. Here, semicolons are used to differentiate statements instead of the colon, which is common to Microsoft BASIC. This same macro substitution process is carried out for each of the swap lines. The last line in the program displays the swapped values on the monitor. You can begin to get an idea of how valuable macros can be by looking at the following C program, which is the equivalent of the first, except that the swapping process is handled by functions.

```
main()
{

        int x, y;
        char *a, *b;
        float i, j, swapf();

        x = 3;
        y = 10;
        a = "HELLO";
        b = "GOODBYE";
        i = 1.219;
        j = 4.6275;

        swapi(&x, &y);
        swaps(a, b);
        swapf(&i, &j);

        printf("%d %d %s %s %f %f\n", x, y, a, b, i, j);

}
```

Program continues

```
swapi(a, b)
int *a, *b;
{

        int c;

        c = *a;
        *a = *b;
        *b = c;

}
swaps(a, b)
char *a, *b;
{

        char *c;

        c = a;
        a = b;
        b = c;

}
float swapf(a, b)
float *a, *b;
{

        float c;

        c = *a;
        *a = *b;
        *b = c;

}
```

This program is similar to the previous one, except the #define line has been removed, and three swap functions have been added. Each is a different function and has a different name. For instance, swapi swaps the values of integers; swaps trades the values of two string variables; and swapf swaps the values of two floating-point variables. You can see that this program is at least twice as long as the previous one and therefore takes quite a bit longer to input via the keyboard. The SWAP statement in Microsoft BASIC is more readily converted to C by the use of macro substitution than by the use of functions.

The following C language program shows another way macro substitutions may be used:

```
#define copy(A, B)   strcat(A, B)
#define prints(A)  printf("%s\n", A);
main()
{

    char *x, *y;

    x = "HELLO";
    y = "GOODBYE";

    copy(x, y);

    prints(x);

}
```

Here, copy is used to replace the strcat function. This applies only when writing the program. When the program is compiled, copy is replaced by strcat. The macro prints is #defined as printf. Therefore, when you type prints(x) in the source program, this is automatically replaced by the printf statement, which will display string x on the screen. These substitutions can go on forever. I think you will find that macros are highly useful when a fairly simple substitution is called for. However, macros are limited in the amount of information that can be crammed into them, and one must remember that macros are not called for when needed in the program as functions are. For example, in our discussion of the pause function, the functions lines were included only once within the program. However, pause( ) was called several times. If pause were handled as a macro substitution each time it was included in the main program, the lines that make up the macro substitution would be written at that location within the program. This could make the compiled program much larger in size than the program equivalent using functions. If program size is a key concern, one must closely examine the use of a macro. If it is used many times, it might be better written as a function.

ASSIGNMENTS

1. Write a function called cube, that receives an integer value and returns the cube of that value.
2. Write a function called the cubef that receives a float value and returns the cube of that value.
3. Write a macro, printi, that displays its argument to the screen.
4. Write a macro, print2, that will display its string argument two times on the screen.

C PROGRAM FORMAT AND MISTAKES

At this point in the discussion, the reader should have gained a fair amount of knowledge about C, its functions, and its relationship to BASIC. It was mentioned earlier that C is a very flexible language, both in what it can do and how the source programs are written. For the most part, C is independent regarding the actual format of the source code. This relates directly to white spaces and the general way the program lines are laid out. All programs in this book have followed the standard C programming format, which will at first seem a bit strange to readers with experience in BASIC only. This chapter will further explore the proper way to write a C language program. Specifically, program examples will be shown in several different "workable" formats. Also, examples of improperly written programs will be given; these examples will address the errors many beginning C programmers make.

The following C language program is written in what might be classified as the standard format. The call to main() begins the program, and main() is written at the left margin. The opening brace is written immediately below main() and also at the left margin. Usually, the first assignment in writing a C language program is to declare all variables. In this example, I have indented five spaces and named x an int. When all variables have been declared, the next step is to assign values to variables. Again, I have indented five spaces and have also skipped a line between the declaration and the assignment. The skipping of a line here is done simply to differentiate between program blocks. The first block is the opening call to main() and its opening brace; the second is the declaration of variables; the third is the assignment of variables. The fourth block in this particular program is the first function line, which is also indented five spaces. A line has been skipped here to differentiate this block from the assignment block.

The end result is a program whose key blocks or elements are clearly defined. C is not always an easy language to understand; but by clearly defining program blocks in this manner, C programs can be more clearly understood.

```
main()
{

    int x;

    x = 5;

    printf("%d\n", x);

}
```

Such formatting is done so that a program you write in C can be more easily understood by someone else. As programs take on more complexity, it's quite easy to lose track of what you've done if you don't follow such a format. Also, since your learning experience will involve reading materials and viewing programs written by others, it's good to get in the habit of writing your programs in the standard format. By doing this, you will become accustomed to the way C programs are normally presented.

From the compiler's point of view, such formatting is totally unnecessary. The above program could just as well have been written as follows:

```
main()
{
    int x;
    x = 5;
    printf("%d\n", x);
}
```

Here, the indentations from the previous program have been maintained. However, the line spacing is not the same. This simple program is still quite easy to understand when presented in this format; but the same will not hold true for a complex program. In this example, no blocks are clearly defined, and everything seems to run together.

The next program example is in a format that many BASIC programmers use when first starting out in C. This format is definitely to be avoided, since it tends to further muddy the waters of source program understanding.

```
main()
{
int x;
x = 5;
printf("%d\n", x);
}
```

In this example, all lines begin at the left margin. Due to the many symbols used in C (braces, brackets, ampersands, and so on), it's quite easy to omit a brace or other symbol and not be able to clearly spot the error. This format may seem more comfortable to a BASIC programmer at first, but it will soon become unwieldy as programming experience increases.

Multiple statement lines are quite common in BASIC. Most dialects of BASIC support multiple statement lines and usually use colons as separators. Multiple statement, or more appropriately, multiple block lines are also permitted in C, as demonstrated by the following program:

```
main()
{
        int x; x = 5; printf("%d\n", x);
}
```

Here, the separators are semicolons. There's no real problem in this example; but one must remember that several C language statements such as *if*, *while*, and *for* are not normally terminated with semicolons; real problems can be encountered when they are included on one line.

As an extreme example, another version of the original program is shown below:

```
main(){ int x; x = 5; printf("%d\n", x); }
```

If you include many lines like this in any C language program, it will probably have meaning only to you.

All of the program examples shown were compiled using the Lattice C-Compiler. No error messages were generated, and all runs were successful. Again, to the compiler, formatting is of no consequence; but to the person learning C, it is absolutely essential for a steady transition from the novice level upward. Each time you write a C language program, compare the finished product with a similar example in this or other books about C. If you notice a format deviation, make the necessary changes so that your program will conform. I'll admit that at first, sticking to this format is difficult because it seems to slow you down. However, after a fairly short period of time, you will automatically begin writing all C language programs using the standard format. In other words, after a bit of practice, this highly useful format becomes quite comfortable.

You certainly have noticed by now that most mathematical operations in C are programmed using white space differentiators between elements. For example, the BASIC program line:

```
X=4*2
```

would appear in a C program as:

```
x = 4 * 2
```

This isn't the case all the time, but it should be. The reason for the use of lower-case letters to name functions, and, for the most part, variables in C, is purely convention. In C, upper-case letters are reserved for symbolic names and constants. Everything else is normally written in lower-case letters. The spacing between the equals sign and the mathematical operators (the asterisk for multiplication in this case) tends to highlight a mathematical operation. Using this format, the asterisk, when used to indicate multiplication, is not readily confused with the asterisk that is used to indicate a pointer. Mathematical operations are sometimes performed on pointers, and it's possible for two asterisks to appear back to back, as in:

```
x=*p**z;
```

This is a little difficult to understand. However,

```
x = *p * *z;
```

provides a little more differentiation, and thus, better clarity.

The following program in C is far more complex than the previous one. Actually, the complexity has more to do with appearance than the actual operation of the program itself. This program is very clearly defined by the C programmer's eye, however, because it follows standard format.

```
main()
{

    int x, y;

    for (x = 0; x <= 100; ++x) {
        y = x * 2;
        printf("%d\n", y);
    }

    while (y <= 0) {
        --y;
        printf("%d\n", y);
    }

}
```

The declarations are handled in an individual block, and there is adequate indentation and line spacing. This program uses two loops using the *for* and *while* statements. Notice that each of the loops is separated by a line, which provides good differentiation. Notice also that the elements of each loop are indented five spaces from the start of the loop statement name. This makes it easy to see which program lines are a part of which loop. You can see that a space follows the *for* and *while* statements before the opening paren. This accentuates the fact that *for* and *while* are C language statements as opposed to functions. In C, the opening paren for a function argument immediately precedes the last letter of the function name. C language statements, however, use a white space following the last letter and the opening paren. Since each loop contains more than one statement, an opening brace follows each argument line. A closing brace marks the end of the loop. You can see that each closing brace is indented five spaces and falls a few lines beneath the first letter of the loop statement. In complex programs, such formatting makes it easier to tell which closing brace is coupled with which loop.

The following program better demonstrates the usefulness of proper closing-brace formatting:

```
main ()
{

     int x, y, z;
     for (x = 0; x <= 100; ++x) {
          y = x * 2;
          printf ("%d\n", y);

          for (z = 0; z <= 20; ++z) {
               z = z * 3;
               printf ("%d\n", z);
          }
     }

}
```

This program uses two loops, one of which is nested. At the end of the first *for* statement line is an opening brace. The same is true of the next *for* statement line, which is a part of the first loop. We know it is a part of the first loop because no closing brace is vertically aligned with the opening *for* statement prior to the inclusion of the second *for* statement. Near the end of the program, you can see three closing braces. It is obvious that the first one is aligned with the nested *for* statement. The next closing brace is vertically aligned with the opening *for* statement. The final closing brace is on the left-hand margin and aligns with the call to main(). Opening and closing braces delineate program blocks, or in BASIC terminology, routines that operate more or less independently. This makes for far easier understanding of a program, because the viewer can quickly break down a complex program into individual blocks and determine the operation of each block on an individual basis.

PROGRAMMING MISTAKES

The next portion of this chapter is a quiz. The reader will be shown several different C language programs, many of which contain errors. However, some are correct as presented. The errors referred to do not involve format, but are of the type that will cause the compiler to generate an error message, and, more than likely, bring about a cessation to execution. The answers are given following each program example.

Problem No. 1:

```
main()
{

    x = 24;

    printf("%d\n", x);


}
```

At first glance, this program may seem to be okay. A close examination of the printf line indicates that everything is in its place. This program is totally incorrect, however, because a variable has been used (x) that has not been previously declared as to type. To make this program executable, the declaration *int x;* must be included prior to $x = 24;$. This is a common mistake, but, fortunately, most compilers will pick up this error and generate an appropriate message telling you what the problem is. Compilation can then be halted in midstream, allowing you to make corrections to the program prior to recompilation. Remember, all variables must be declared prior to their use in a C language program. Sometimes, you may add variables during a programming sequence. These are additional variables that were not previously declared. This is often done with the intention of returning to the declaration block and adding them. All too often, this step is forgotten. Again, the compiler error message should indicate that one or more variables have not been declared. More than likely, the compiler will also indicate which program lines contain the undeclared variables.

Problem No. 2:

```
main()
{

    int x, y;

    x = 1.2;
    y = 44;

    printf("%d %d\n", x, y);

}
```

There is definitely an error in this program, although it's one that most compilers will not catch. Both variables have been declared, and the printf line is
in proper order. However, both variables have been declared as int types, and
variable x has been assigned a floating-point value of 1.2. This program will
execute under most compilers, but the value of x will be converted to an
integer. Therefore, x will be equal to 1 instead of the intended 1.2. This program is corrected by declaring only y an int type and declaring x a float. The
printf statement line must also be modified. The first %d designation must
be changed to %f to indicate conversion to a floating-point value. Problems
of this type create the most difficulty, since the compiler does not usually
indicate the error. In complex programs, such an error can mean hours of
debugging, since what is intended to be a floating-point value is being fed to
other program portions as an integer. When this bogus integer is passed to
other programming formulas, the resulting output answer is incorrect, and
it may not be obvious as to just where the problem lies. A similar experience
occurs when a special function is written that is intended to return a floating-
point value and it is not previously declared a float function. Most of the
time, the arguments will be worked through the function; but an integer
value is always returned.

Problem No. 3:

```
main()

    int x, y, z;

    x = 13;
    y = 2 * x;
    z = y - 1;

    printf("%d %d %d\n", x, y, z);

}
```

The problem with this program may be obvious to many, but to many more it will not. Depending on the compiler, several different error messages may be generated, none of which will clearly define exactly what the problem is. Looking at the program, we can see that all variables have been declared. It would also seem that proper assignments to these variables have been made. Also, there is no problem with the printf line. The problem is a simple one. The opening brace following main() has not been included. This throws the whole program out of whack. More than likely, your compiler will simply halt and indicate that compilation has been terminated. Alternately, every program line may be listed as being an error. The entire situation is corrected by simply adding an opening brace immediately following main(). Remember, error-checking in most C compilers is done on a very rudimentary basis. In many instances, the true nature of the error is defined; but in others, the compiler goes on its best assumption, which is often incorrect. After a bit of experience with a specific compiler, however, you will begin to identify certain error messages with certain program errors. It takes a while to learn this, however, so these problematical exercises should be helpful in speeding along your transition from BASIC to C.

Problem No. 4:

```
main()
{

    int x;

    scanf("%d", x);
    printf("%d\n", x);


}
```

Here is a simple program that allows you to input an integer via the keyboard and then print the integer to the screen. The program, however, is incorrect. Some compilers will catch this; many will not. The error here is the one most often made when using the scanf function. When scanf is used to retrieve a number, the holding variable (in this case, x) must be preceded by an ampersand to indicate its memory location. The variable must be a pointer, and the exclusion of the ampersand means it is not. Therefore, this program will not execute properly, even if it makes it through the compilation process. A correction is made by simply preceding variable x in the scanf line with an ampersand (&).

Problem No. 5:

```
main()
{

    int x, y, z;

    for (x = 0; x <= 14; ++x) {
        y = 2 * x;
        z = 3 * y;
        printf("%d %d %d\n", x, y, z);

}
```

This program uses the *for* loop, which steps *x* from 0 to 14. The elements within the loop assign variables *y* and *z* appropriate values and then print the values of *x*, *y*, and *z* to the screen. The error found in this program will most likely cause your compiler to generate an error message. Using the Lattice C-Compiler, the message will be "unexpected end of file." This means that the program terminated before the compiler expected it to. To help you find the error here, let me give you a clue. Look at the braces. In this program, you will see a total of three braces. This is an automatic error, since braces come in pairs. Whenever there is an opening brace, there must also be a closing brace. What's happened here is that an opening brace was used following the *for* statement line. No closing brace was included at the end of the loop elements. The closing brace at the end of the program is apparently paired with the opening brace following main() (because of its format position in the program). However, the C-compiler treats this last closing brace as the one that matches the opening brace following the *for* statement line. The compiler thinks you included a closing brace following the *for* statement elements, but forgot to include a closing brace matched with the opening one following main(). If you did include a closing brace following the loop and forgot to include a program termination brace, the same error message would be generated. This program can be fixed by simply adding one more closing brace at the end of the program. But to follow proper C programming format, the closing brace to the *for* loop should precede the left margin closing brace and be indented five spaces. This will align it vertically with the opening *for* statement.

Anytime you complete a C language program, especially one that uses a lot of braces, you should perform a quick check to make certain that you always have an even number of braces. If you end up with an odd number, then you've omitted a closing brace or added an unneeded opening brace. This situation must be corrected before a successful compiler run and execution can be obtained.

Problem No. 6:

```
main()
{

    int x;

    while (x < 100)
        ++x;


}
```

This program is intended to count x from 0 to 100 using a *while* loop. It won't work, however, because of a serious error quite common to BASIC programmers making the transition to C. The glaring error here is found in the fact that an initial value of x has not been made. We don't have to do this in BASIC, since a variable is always equal to 0 if it has not been previously assigned. This is not true in C. As a matter of fact, in this example, x can be equal to anything within the range of legal integer values. To make this program work properly, an assignment line must precede the *while* loop setting x to its initial or starting value. The compiler won't catch this error in most instances, and you can never be sure just what value an unassigned variable will assume. Remember, a *for* loop assigns its stepping variable within the loop commands, but a *while* loop of this type must use a variable that has already been assigned a value within the main body of the C program.

This type of error can be quite perplexing, especially if the initial value of x assigned by the computer (as opposed to within a program) falls somewhere within the legal test range of the *while* loop. This means that the count might start midway between the intended beginning and ending points. If the computer-assigned variable value lies outside of the legal test range of the *while* loop, the loop terminates. Remember, assign all variables before they are used, or the computer will assign them with bogus values that have no meaning whatsoever as far as the intention of your program is concerned.

Problem No. 7:

```
main()
{

    int x;

    for (x = 0; x =< 50; ++x)
        printf("%d\n", x);


}
```

You may have to look hard to discover the error in this program. Some compilers may not even see an error, and the program may run fine. However, there is an error of intent here, and it can be found in the second portion of the *for* statement line. Specifically, the problem lies with $x = < 50$. In C, the evaluation for this type of assignment must include the "less than" symbol first, followed by the equals sign. This is not true in BASIC, where we can legally specify "equal to or less than." In C, it is always "less than or equal to." In most instances, this type of error will cause early termination of the loop. Remember that in C, the equals sign always comes last.

Problem No. 8:

```
main()
{

        int x;

        x = 0;

        while (x <= 100) {
                ++x;
                if (x = 50)
                        printf("Variable x equals fifty\n");
        }

}
```

As pointed out earlier in this portion of the chapter, many of the program examples will contain errors, but some will not. I'll bet you think this one doesn't contain any errors. Wrong! This one contains a very serious error. It is serious because most compilers won't catch it; and it can create havoc during the program run. If you are a beginning C programmer, chances are you just can't find the error. The error is found in the *if* statement line, specifically with $x = 50$. One must remember that in C, there are two types of equals operators. The single equals sign (=) is the assignment operator. It assigns the value on the right to the variable on the left. The comparison operator is two equals signs (==). This means that the values on either side of the comparison operator are evaluated. This is what we want in the *if* statement line. As written, the *if* statement test is always true, because x is assigned a value of 50. To make this program run properly, you must change the assignment operator to the double equals comparison operator. Then the value of x will be compared with 50 instead of x being assigned a value of 50. Again, this is a serious error because the compiler won't indicate a problem, and the program will be executable. However, it will not execute in the manner intended. In BASIC, there is only one equals symbol, and it is used for both assignment and comparison. Unintentionally replacing the comparison operator with the assignment operator in C is a common mistake made by many beginning C language programmers.

Problem No. 9:

```
main()
{

    int x;
    float y;
    char *c;

    scanf("%d %s %f", &x, &c, &y);
    printf("%s %f %d\n", c, y, x);

}
```

This simple program uses the scanf function to retrieve an integer, a string, and a floating-point number from the keyboard input. The printf function is then used to display all three values. There is an error in this program, and it involves the scanf line. All variables have been properly declared, and ampersands have preceded each one in the scanf line. However, we do not use an ampersand to precede a char * value or a character array value. These are already pointers. Only the numeric variables declared as float, int, double, and so on need to provide pointers (by inclusion of the ampersand) in scanf arguments. With some compilers, you can get away with including an ampersand preceding a character array variable, but not with a char * value. In any event, neither a char * value nor a character array value should be preceded by the ampersand when used with scanf. In this case, the compiler will probably perform its conversions without any error messages, and the executable program will seem to run properly until an attempt is made to print the value of *c* in this example. Chances are it will come up blank. The program is corrected by removing the ampersand preceding variable *c* in the scanf line.

Problem No. 10:

```
main()
{

    printf("Hello,\nHow are you?\nI am fine.");

}
```

This program is used to print phrases on the screen. At first glance, it appears quite odd, but in reality there's nothing wrong with this program. It is correct as shown. This program will display:

Hello,
How are you?
I am fine.

We are accustomed to seeing the backslash *n* newline character at the end of a quoted phrase or conversion specifier. This, however, is not mandatory. A newline character may occur anywhere within the quoted string, and at this point, the carriage is returned, and a new line is generated. This single printf statement line takes the place of three printf statement lines—the first two terminated by newline characters and the last one not. Again, this program is correct and should compile and execute prefectly.

Problem No. 11:

```
main()
{

    int x, y;

    x = 23;
    y = 27;

    printf("The numbers are %d %d"\n, x, y);

}
```

This program prints the phrase "The numbers are" followed by the values of *x* and *y*. As written, though, the program will generate an error message because of a problem in the printf line. This illustrates another common mistake made by many beginning C programmers. Note that the quoted phrase and the conversion specifiers are contained within quotation marks. However, the terminating newline character (backslash *n*) is found outside the quotation marks. This is incorrect. The newline character has the same significance as any other character and must be included within quotation marks. The program is corrected by inserting the final quotation mark following the newline character.

Problem No. 12:

```
main ()
{

    char *c;

    c = "COMPUTER";

    printf(%s "is the word\n", c);

}
```

You probably spotted the problem with this program almost immediately due to the discussion about the previous program. The problem here also lies in the printf line. The conversion specifier (%s) is contained outside the quotation marks. Like the newline character, the conversion specifier must be included within the quotation marks. In BASIC, we are not accustomed to seeing arguments or variables included as part of a quoted phrase line. However, in C, they are intermingled. This program is corrected by inserting the opening quotation mark prior to the conversion specification.

Problem No. 13:

```
main ()
{

    int x, y, z;
    char *c;

    x = 43;
    y = 2 * x;
    z = 2 * y;
    c = "Hello";

    printf("%d %s %d %d\n", x, y, c, z);

}
```

This C language program uses three int variables and one string pointer, which are duly assigned proper values. The printf function is used to display each on the monitor screen. This program, however, does have an error—one that will not be caught by most compilers. Look at the conversion specifiers in the printf line. The first one indicates an integer value and indeed, variable x has been declared an integer. The second specifier indicates a character string value, but its matching variable (y) is an integer. The next specifier names an integer, but its matching variable (c) has been declared a string pointer. This mistake is the result of a simple typing error. Obviously, the programmer intended for variable c to be matched with the %s conversion specification. If this program were executed as shown, erroneous screen data would be displayed due to the mismatch. The extent of the erroneous display would depend on the type of compiler and the computer itself. This program is corrected by reversing variables c and y in the printf line.

Problem No. 14:

```
main()
{

    int x;

    x = 43;

    print("%d\n", x);

}
```

At first glance, this program appears to be perfect. A programmer who had never learned BASIC and was beginning to learn C would probably spot the error immediately. The error in this program is aimed directly at BASIC programmers, who may tend to overlook it. Variable x has been properly declared an int. It has also been properly assigned an integer value. Therefore, the problem must lie in the next line. Look closely. Instead of printf, a standard C function, "print" has been used. The compiler will look for a personalized function named "print" and generate an error message. With the Lattice C-Compiler, this type of error would not generate an error message. However, when the object file generated by the compiler is passed through the linker, upon output of the executable program, the linker will generate an error message "UNRESOLVED EXTERNAL DEFINITION." This means the linker could not find a function named "print" in the C library file. What you end up with is an executable program that won't do anything. Obviously, the program is corrected by changing "print" to printf.

Problem No. 15:

```
main()
{

    int x;
    char *c;

    c = "Diskette";
    x = strlen(c)

    printf("%d\n", x);

}
```

This last problem contains a very simple and common error, although it may not be obvious at first glance. When compiling this program, most compilers will generate an error message that would indicate the line immediately following the error line contains a miscue. The error message will be "omission of semicolon," or something similar. Indeed, a semicolon has been omitted at the end of the line that uses strlen. With some compilers, this is not a fatal error. The compiler may add that missing semicolon for you. In others, the compiler may crash. Remember, a semicolon following a function converts that function to a program statement line. This program is corrected by simply adding a semicolon at the end of the strlen line.

SUMMARY

This chapter has dealt with two subject areas that are crucial to the beginning C language programmer. Proper program formatting is absolutely essential in order to gain a clear understanding of C programming from the onset. To stray substantially from this format is to invite disaster in the form of a slow complex learning process and an unclear understanding of what is taking place within a given program. Using a non-standard format may suffice for your own personal needs, but it will tend to blur comprehension and make your programs almost useless to those who may want to learn from you. Proper adherence to the standard C language format is not mandatory from a compilation and execution point of view, but it is mandatory that you follow it in order to go as far as you possibly can in learning to program in C.

Beginning as well as seasoned programmers will always make certain errors when writing C programs. However, beginners tend to make program-

ming errors that fall into the category of syntax errors. These are easily
spotted by the experienced programmer, but are difficult for the beginner
to detect. This chapter has dealt with some of the most common programming errors made by beginners, and it is hoped that the examples presented
will allow you to be on the alert for similar errors in your programs. The
error messages generated by your compiler are a help, but often, these messages are crude "guesstimates" of the real problem. Fortunately, beginning
C programmers usually write a large number of very short, simple programs
at the onset. By detecting bugs in these small programs, the syntactical
problems usually do not carry over to the more complex programs that are
written after a bit of practical experience of programming in C has been
obtained.

CHARACTERS, CONVERSION, AND CONFUSION

This chapter is appropriately named and alludes to the three C's of going from BASIC to C. The way C utilizes individual characters has no direct corresponding use in BASIC. Likewise, conversions in C usually require no specialized functions as they do in BASIC. The third part of the three C's is confusion, and it is the author's hope that this book will help to eliminate most of yours.

In BASIC, we are primarily concerned with two types of variables, numeric and string. Certainly, numeric variables can be broken down into integer, floating-point, and double-precision types. However, we have no such sub-categories when dealing with string variables. In BASIC, a string variable may be used to hold a single number, a single letter, or a string of letters, numbers, or a combination of both. The same is true in C, but C goes a few steps further and adds different variable types under what might be a major classification of "string" variables. As in BASIC, a character string pointer may be assigned a numeric value or an alphanumeric value. This value may consist of one or more characters. However, C also offers a *char* variable (as opposed to a char * or char array variable). Anytime you want a variable to contain a single character, you may declare a variable as *char* and use that variable to contain the character or the ASCII code of the character. In C, a char variable is handled like an integer. As a matter of fact, when you assign a specific character (by name) to a char variable, that variable contains the ASCII code of the character.

BASIC Language:

```
10   CH$ = "A"
20   PRINT CH$
```

This simple BASIC program assigns to string variable CH$ a value of "A." CH$ is then displayed on the screen using the PRINT statement.

C Language:

```
main()
{

        char ch;

        ch = 'A';

        printf("%c\n", ch);

}
```

This is one possible equivalent of the previous program in BASIC using a char variable in C. We could also have used a character pointer. But why do this when a char variable will suffice? First, *ch* is declared a char type. This variable is assigned a value in the next line. Here, the constant "A" is assigned as a single character. This is done using the apostrophe in place of the quotation marks. This means that *ch* is now equal to the character "A", or more accurately, *ch* is equal to the ASCII code (65) of the letter "A". The ASCII code is assigned from the computer set.

The printf function is used with a new type of conversion specification. The designator %c indicates that a character is to be printed (as opposed to a character string, floating-point value, or decimal integer). When the program is run, the capital letter "A" will be displayed on the screen.

BASIC Language:

```
10   CH$ = "A"
20   PRINT ASC(CH$)
```

This BASIC program uses the ASC function to cause the ASCII code of the first character contained in CH$ to be displayed on the screen. Since CH$ contains only one character, the letter "A," its ASCII code (65) will be displayed.

C Language:

```
main()
{

    char ch;

    ch = 'A';

    printf("%d\n", ch);

}
```

In C, there is no function equivalent to the ASC function in BASIC, because none is really needed. As stated earlier, char types are treated just like int types for most operations, so conversion from character to ASCII code of character is handled within the printf line only. This program is identical to the previous C program, except for the conversion specification in the printf line. We are supplying variable *ch* as the argument to the printf function line. We already know that *ch* has been declared a char type. However, the conversion specification (%d) indicates that the value is to be displayed as an integer. Therefore, the integer value of *ch* (ASCII 65) is displayed on the screen.

BASIC Language:

```
10  X% = 65
20  PRINT CHR$(X%)
```

This BASIC program uses the CHR$ function to print the character whose ASCII value is contained in X%. ASCII code 65 represents the capital letter "A." Therefore, the CHR$ function will display "A" on the screen. screen.

C Language:

```
main()
{

    int x;

    x = 65;

    printf("%c\n", x);

}
```

As was the case with the ASC function, there is no specialized function in C to convert a number to its character equivalent. None is necessary. In this program, x is declared an int type and is assigned a value of 65. Again, the conversion is carried out using the printf function. The conversion specification used here (%c) means that a character is to be printed. The ASCII code of the character is contained in int variable x, which serves as the argument for printf. Therefore, the character represented by ASCII 65 (capital letter "A") is displayed on the screen.

To further illustrate the tie between char types and int types, the following C language program does exactly what the previous C program did:

```
main()
{

    char x;

    x = 65;

    printf("%c\n", x);

}
```

Here, x is declared a char type and is then assigned the integer value of 65. The printf function uses a character conversion specification and char x as its argument. Again, the letter "A" is displayed on the screen. Therefore, we know that a char type can be assigned a single character value by enclosing that character in apostrophes. It may also be assigned an integer value (0–255). Remember, even when a character type is assigned to a char variable, the variable actually receives the ASCII value of that character. There's nothing unusual about a char type being able to accept an integer value.

As discussed in Chapter 3, putchar can be used to display a single character on the screen, and getchar may be used to retrieve a single character from the keyboard. However, putchar will always output the character itself. It cannot be used to convert a character to its ASCII code value. Putchar can, however, be used to convert an ASCII value assigned to an int variable or a char variable to its character equivalent.

The scanf function can also be used to retrieve a character from the console when used in the format of:

```
scanf("%c", &x);
```

where x has been declared a char type.

To avoid confusion, it's usually best to use a char variable anytime you need a variable to hold a single character or possibly an ASCII code of a character. While char types can effectively be used in place of int types, and indeed, they are in certain specialized functions, this practice can cause confusion for the beginner.

BASIC Language:

```
10  I% = 255
20  PRINT HEX$(I%)
```

This BASIC program uses the HEX$ function to print the hexadecimal value of the decimal value contained in I%. The HEX$ function will return the hexadecimal equivalent of decimal 255 in this example, which is "FF."

C Language:

```
main()
{

        int i;

        i = 255;

        printf("%x\n", i);

}
```

As you may have realized by now, there is no equivalent of the HEX$ function in C. Again, none is needed. The conversion is accomplished using the printf function and the hexadecimal conversion specification (%x). The decimal value in variable *i* is converted to hexadecimal form being displayed on the screen. The displayed value will again be "FF."

BASIC Language:

```
10  I% = 255
20  PRINT OCT$(I%)
```

This BASIC program uses the OCT$ function to print the octal value of I% on the screen. The octal value of decimal 255 is 377. This is the number that will be displayed.

C Language:

```
main()
{

    int i;

    i = 255;

    printf("%o\n", i);

}
```

Again, the printf function is used to make the needed conversion from decimal to octal in this example. The octal conversion specification (%o) is used to convert the decimal value of *i* to its octal equivalent of 377 before being displayed on the screen. The octal conversion specification is represented by "percent-oh" as opposed to "percent-zero."

The scanf function may be used to receive hexadecimal or octal values via the keyboard, as in:

```
scanf("%x", &i);      "HEXADECIMAL"
scanf("%o", &i);      "OCTAL"
```

Remember to include the ampersand before each variable. All variables should previously have been declared as int types. As in BASIC, integers may be decimal, hexadecimal, or octal in base. Also, we may make assignments directly to int variables in hexadecimal or octal notation. Hexadecimal notation in BASIC requires the value be preceded by "&H". This indicates that the value is hexadecimal. In C, a similar prefix is required to indicate a hexadecimal value; but in this case, it's "0x" (zero-x). Here, I'm referring to the letter "x" preceded by zero. The letter x is a character as opposed to a variable. The prefix notation for octal constants is simply the character zero. The following lines demonstrate such assignments:

```
int x, y;
x = 0xb800;        "HEXADECIMAL ASSIGNMENT"
y = 0377;          "OCTAL ASSIGNMENT"
```

SUMMARY

While this chapter is short, it hopefully will clear up some of the misunderstandings that are picked up by BASIC programmers making the transition to C. When first starting out in C, it seems that nearly everything you do is far more difficult than it is in BASIC. This would give the impression that C is a far more difficult language than BASIC. This is totally untrue. The C programming language is simply much more versatile than BASIC. We've already seen that performing numeric conversions is quite simple, and there is a brand new variable type (char) that can be used to hold single characters or integers. Most of the difficulty encountered by BASIC programmers making the transition to C lies in the preconceived prejudices that have been garnered by using BASIC exclusively. I have seen many BASIC programmers laboriously convert hexadecimal numbers to decimal notation in order to input these values in C programs. (Incidentally, these conversions were made using the HEX$ function on a separate computer running under BASIC.) As you know, numeric variables in BASIC can directly be assigned hexadecimal numbers; but for some reason, these programmers thought the same was not true in C. C language does not offer all of the conveniences found in BASIC statements through its standard set of functions; but operationally, C is an easier language to use and the equivalents of these BASIC functions can usually be programmed quickly (if necessary at all). Examples of mimicking BASIC statements and functions in C have already been provided, and more will follow.

The gist of this chapter is, "Try not to treat new variable types or conversion methods as problems, but rather as bonuses only C can offer." In the long run, these bonuses will make programming in C a much more pleasant experience. As a matter of fact, whenever you return to BASIC, you undoubtedly will begin to miss the flexibility of C.

CHAPTER 9

MIMICKING BASIC STATEMENTS AND FUNCTIONS IN C

In previous chapters, we have learned how C functions are built and called from C programs. A function is simply a C language program that may or may not require the passing of argument values and is begun by listing its name. The function is then called by name from a C language program. If a programmer knows that there will be a continuous need for a certain routine that is not offered as part of the standard C language function set, he or she will build that function and include it with any programs that will have need of it. (It was stated earlier that anything offered by BASIC can be duplicated in C.) One of the main reasons that some of the BASIC functions and statements are not included as part of the standard C function set is the purpose of C itself. C was designed to be a transportable language. This means that a program can be written in C on one machine and then passed to another. The latter machine would run the program in the same way the former did. Many statements and functions in BASIC are machine-dependent. For instance, you won't find the equivalent of a CLS statement in C because the process of clearing the computer screen is a machine-dependent one. It will depend on the type of computer, the type of display board the computer contains, the screen buffer memory location, and several other factors. About the closest we can come to CLS in C and still maintain its portability is a *for* loop that contains a printf statement with a newline character in quotation marks. Each time the loop cycles, a new line is generated. This effectively scrolls any information off the visible screen. It's not as efficient as CLS, but it is a transportable routine that will work on all computers programmed under C.

The CLS statement can be duplicated for any computer in C, but there's a good chance that the function that is built will work on only one type of machine or the host machine and those that are closely compatible with it.

This chapter will discuss some of the more commonly used BASIC language statements and functions and show how they can be duplicated in C language functions. Most of the functions presented here are not as efficient as they could be because they are written with concern for the reader's understanding them rather than machine efficiency. As you learn more about C, you will also learn that some of the most efficient C language programs may also be the most difficult to decipher, especially for the beginner or the programmer with moderate experience. All of these functions should be transportable and will work as described on any machine that can be programmed in C.

BASIC Statement:

INPUT

The INPUT statement in BASIC is used to retrieve information via the keyboard. The type of information is dependent upon the variable that follows INPUT. For instance, INPUT A$ indicates that INPUT is expecting a string input that may consist of numbers, alphabetic characters, or a combination of both.

C Function:

scanf
gets
getchar

Any of these three functions can be used to return a keyboard value in the same manner as INPUT. Scanf may be used to retrieve any type of value, depending on its specifications. Gets probably comes closest to matching INPUT because it will accept a string value that may later be converted to a floating-point number or an integer if applicable. Getchar is used to retrieve a single character via the keyboard. All of these functions require that the RETURN key be pressed after entering the information.

BASIC Program:

```
10 INPUT A$
20 PRINT A$
```

This program uses the INPUT statement to retrieve a string value from the keyboard. The PRINT statement is then used to display the value on the screen.

C Language:

```
main()
{

        char *a;

        inputs(a);

        printf("%s\n", a);

}
inputs(c)
char *c;
{

        gets(c);

}
```

One might say that I have gone the long way around on this C language version, but it does demonstrate how a statement in BASIC may be reproduced as a function in C. First, *a* is declared a string pointer The personalized function is called *inputs*, which stands for "input a string." I could have called it anything I wanted, as long as the name did not conflict with the standard C language function set. All the function uses is the standard gets function in C to retrieve the string value from the keyboard. Basically, all this function does is use inputs to replace the standard gets function. As a matter of fact, the program would have been much more efficient if we dropped the personalized function completely and, prior to main( ), included a preprocessor macro definition such as:

#define   inputs(X)   gets(X)

The rest of the program would remain as presented, except that the inputs function at the end is dropped completely.

However, the INPUT statement in BASIC may also include a screen prompt.

BASIC Language:

```
10  INPUT "TYPE ANY STRING VALUE"; A$
20  PRINT A$
```

This program includes a screen prompt, which is contained in quotation marks immediately following the INPUT statement.

C Language:

```
main()
{

    char *a;

    inputs("TYPE ANY STRING VALUE", a);

    printf("%s", a);

}
inputs(m, s)
char *m, *s;
{

    printf("%s ", m);
    gets(s);

}
```

The inputs function in this program duplicates exactly the INPUT statement in the previous BASIC program, with the exception that the flashing question mark (?) prompt won't appear as it does in Microsoft BASIC. Notice that the call to inputs in the program has enclosed the prompt message in quotation marks within the parens that contain the arguments. Char * variable a is included as the second argument for inputs. The prompt message is the first argument. Looking at the function itself (toward the bottom of the program), we can see that variable m represents the message argument, while s represents the string variable. Both variables are declared as char * types within the function. Then, the printf function is used to display the value of m, which is the prompt message. The gets function is used to retrieve a string value from the keyboard and assign it to string variable s. When the function returns control to the main program, variable a is now equal to the keyboard input. The printf function displays the input on the screen.

Again, this function could be replaced by a preprocessor macro definition. To do this, simply drop the inputs function portion of the program and, preceding main( ), type:

```
#define   inputs(X, Y)   printf("%s ", X); gets(Y);
```

You must remember, however, that when a macro is defined, it is substituted in the program each time inputs is called. If inputs is called many times, it would be far more efficient from the standpoint of program size to use the function. Either way, the INPUT statement in BASIC is mimicked for string values.

BASIC Language:

```
10  X% = -12
20  PRINT ABS(X%)
```

This program uses the ABS function in BASIC, which returns the absolute value of a number. In this case, the PRINT statement will display the absolute value of -12, which is 12, or +12. Absolute values are always positive numbers. In C compilers, you will sometimes find an ABS function. The Lattice C-Compiler (Version 2.0) does contain such a function. Other compilers, however, may not offer this. No problem. It's a very simple matter to build one.

C Language:

```
main()
{

        int x;

        x = -12;

        printf("%d\n", abs(x));

}
abs(i)
int i;
{

        if (i < 0)
                return(-i);

        return(i);

}
```

This program does the same thing as the BASIC program. The abs function found near the bottom of the program uses an *if* statement to test for the argument value found in *i* being equal to a value which is less than 0. This indicates a negative number. Therefore, the *return* statement coupled with the *if* statement line returns -*i*. When *i* is already negative, as in -12, then -(-12) is equal to +12. This first *return* statement is executed only when *i* is less than 0. The *return* statement automatically returns control to the main program. On the other hand, if the *if* test proves negative (that is, *i* is equal to or more than 0), the second *return* statement is executed. This simply returns the original value of *i*.

Another method of writing the ABS function is shown below:

```
abs(i)
int i;
{

    return(i < 0 ? -i : i);

}
```

I realize that this function, or rather its format, will look quite alien to you at this juncture. However, all this line says is if *i* is less than 0, return -*i*; *else* return *i*. This function uses the "? :" operators, which in BASIC terminology can be taken to mean "THEN" and "ELSE", respectively. Here, the *if* statement is assumed. This single line is exactly equivalent to:

```
if (i < 0)
        return(-i);
else
        return(i);
```

The question mark and colon operators can effectively be used to speed program input time. They can be used almost anywhere for improved programming efficiency. Take the following, for example:

```
printf("%d", i == 0 ? i : j);
```

In this printf line, the value of variable *i* is printed when *i* is equal to 0; *else* the value of *j* is printed. Many new C language programmers do not take advantage of the programming speed and versatility offered by these operators. They allow you to stick in an *if-else* test anywhere you want to.

The abs function in C is a prime candidate for implementation as a macro. You can delete the function altogether and precede main( ) with:

```
#define   abs(I)    ((I) < 0 ? -(I) : (I))
```

This will allow you to use abs in the same way the function did.

BASIC Language:

```
10 J% = 4 ^ 2
20 PRINT J%
```

This program assigns J% the value of 4 squared using the exponentiation symbol. This value is displayed on the screen. An exponentiation function is not part of the standard C language function set, although some compilers may offer it as a specialized function often named power( ). We can easily build such a function in C as long as we only desire to raise numbers to an integer power. Before we move on to the C language program, let's build a subroutine in BASIC that will do the same thing.

```
10 J% = 4
20 GOSUB 100
30 PRINT K%
40 END
100 K% = 1
110 FOR X% = 1 TO 2
120 K% = K% * J%
130 NEXT X%
140 RETURN
```

The subroutine beginning at line 100 is set up to assign to K% the square of J%. The loop determines the number of times that K% is multiplied by J%. In this case, the number is 2, since we wish to arrive at a square. On the first pass of the loop, K% is, initially, equal to 1. Therefore, in line 120, K% is equal to 1 times J%. On the second and final pass of the loop, K% is equal to itself, which is now the same value as J% times J%. Since J% times J% is the same as J% squared, K% is now equal to J% squared. Here's a more versatile method:

```
10 J% = 4
20 P% = 6
30 GOSUB 100
40 PRINT K%
50 END
100 K% = 1
110 FOR X% = 1 to P%
120 K% = K% * J%
130 NEXT X%
140 RETURN
```

This program assigns to J% the value to be raised to a power (4). Integer variable P% contains the power to which J% is to be raised (6). Both of these values are used in the subroutine. In this example, the loop in line 110 will cycle six times. At the end of the loop, K% will be equal to J% raised to the power of P%, or 4 raised to the power of 6. This latter example is quite similar to the way the power function is built in C.

C Language:

```
main()
{

    int j;

    j = power(4, 2);

    printf("%d\n", j);

}
power(x, r)
int x, r;
{

    int a, b;

    b = 1;
    for (a = 1; a <= r; ++a)
        b = b * x;

    return(b);

}
```

In this example, the power function is used with two arguments. The first is the root number; the second is the exponent. You can see that in the function itself, the same sequence of lines is used as in the previous BASIC program. Two new variables are declared within the function, a and b, and b is assigned an initial value of 1. Variable a is incremented in the *for* loop from 1 to the value of r, which represents the exponent in the original function call. Variable b is multiplied by x, which is the root value passed by the function call. When the loop times out, variable b is equal to the root raised to the specified power (in this case, 2).

This program is applicable only to integer root values and to integer exponents. It's a simple matter to allow this function to return float or double values, however, by simply passing a floating-point argument as the root. But, the exponent must still remain an integer value (positive). Raising numbers to negative exponent values or to floating-point exponent values is another matter altogether. This involves complex formulas and approximations that are not within the scope of this discussion. These would be required, however, to duplicate exactly the exponentiation operations of Microsoft BASIC.

BASIC Language:

```
10 D$ = "MICROPROCESSOR"
20 B$ = LEFT$(D$,5)
30 PRINT B$
```

This program uses the LEFT$ function in Microsoft BASIC, which returns the specified leftmost characters of a string. In this example, B$ will be equal to "MICRO," the five leftmost characters in "MICROPROCESSOR." The standard C language function set does not contain the equivalent of the LEFT$ function, but it's a fairly simple matter to build one. However, to do so, we must think of the way that strings are actually stored. This applies to both BASIC and C, but in BASIC, we tend to think of a string variable as containing a quantity that can only be manipulated with functions like LEFT$, RIGHT$, MID$, and so on. In C, we can treat character pointer values a bit differently. Before moving on to the C program, let's build the LEFT$ function in BASIC. To do so requires a slightly different approach than you may be accustomed to. In C, a character string is treated like an array, with each array element containing a letter of the string. The BASIC example follows:

```
10 DIM D$(14)
20 D$(1) = "M"
30 D$(2) = "I"
40 D$(3) = "C"
50 D$(4) = "R"
60 D$(5) = "O"
70 D$(6) = "P"
80 D$(7) = "R"
90 D$(8) = "O"
100 D$(9) = "C"
110 D$(10) = "E"
120 D$(11) = "S"
130 D$(12) = "S"
140 D$(13) = "O"
150 D$(14) = "R"
160 GOSUB 1000
170 PRINT B$
180 END
1000 FOR X% = 1 TO 5
1010 B$ = B$ + D$(X%)
1020 NEXT X%
1030 RETURN
```

This Rube Goldberg method of extrapolating the five leftmost characters of the D$ array looks quite strange, but, in reality, this is the way the LEFT$ function really works on a machine level. In C, one must often think of character pointer variables as one character array that contains the total value on a character-by-character basis, each assigned to a different sequential array element. In C, we have character pointer variables and character arrays. For most operations, both may be treated identically when used in functions.

C Language:

```
main()
{

        char *b, *d;

        d = "MICROPROCESSOR";
        left(b, d, 5);

        printf("%s\n", b);

}
left(a, c, i)
char *a, *c;
int i;
{

        int x;

        for (x = 1; x <= i; ++x)
                *a++ = *c++;

}
```

The left function contains three arguments. The first is the variable that will be assigned the leftmost characters. The second variable (d) contains the value (MICROPROCESSOR). The third argument specifies the number of characters to be passed to b. Incidentally, the last argument is specified here as a constant, but it can just as easily be a variable (int) that has been assigned the number of leftmost characters to be retrieved.

In the function itself, things seem to get complicated, but not so much if you think of *a and *c as two arrays. The positions of each can be assigned a single character. In the function, *c is the variable that contains the word MICROPROCESSOR. Char pointer variable *a will be passed the leftmost characters specified by the integer value. Now for a little more discussion on the increment operator "++". We have used this operator mainly in *for* loops, but in every case, the operator has preceded the variable, as in "++x." When the incrementing operator follows a variable (of any type), an incrementation takes place. However, when the operator precedes the variable, the incrementation takes place *before* the variable is used. When it follows the variable, incrementation takes place *after* the variable is used. This is demonstrated below:

10 X = X + 1 : PRINT X

This is the BASIC version of the C language line:

printf ("%d", ++x);

Here, x is incremented, and its value is then displayed. Another use is shown below in BASIC format:

10 PRINT X : X = X + 1

This is the BASIC version of the C language line:

printf ("%d", x++);

In this case, the value of x is displayed and *then* incremented. In both examples, x is incremented by 1, but in the first example, it was incremented and then used. In the second, it was used and then incremented.

Let's return now to the left function. When character pointers are used in this manner, $*c$ points to the first character in the word MICROPROCESSOR, which is its value. Likewise, $*c$++ points to the first character. However, when the incrementing operator immediately after $*a$ points to the first character, the ++ causes it to be stepped by 1; so the next use of $*c$++ means that $*c$ points to the second character in the value (i) and is then incremented to point to the third character on the next use.

As in the BASIC program, a *for* loop is created that counts from 1 to the value of i, which is 5 in this case. The statement executed in the *for* loop is:

*a++ = *c++

Therefore, on the first pass of the loop, the first position in a is equal to the first character in c. When this assignment is made, $*a$ is incremented by 1, which points to the second character position. Likewise, $*c$ is incremented by 1 and points to the second character in its value. This process continues until the loop times out. This occurs when the fifth character, as designated by i, has been passed to a. The function then returns control to the calling program, and b is now equal to the first five characters in d. Remember, b and d in the main program are equivalent to a and c in the function.

The next C program works identically to the previous one. As a matter of fact, the program *is* identical on a line-by-line basis, except for the function portion. Notice that instead of defining *a* and *b* as string pointers, they are defined as character arrays. Normally, the brackets that follow a character array variable must contain an integer that defines the number of array elements. However, in a function such as this one, or at any time a value is to be passed or assigned to a character array, the element size may be omitted. The compiler will work with the size of the value passed or assigned to the array and dimension it accordingly.

Undoubtedly, you are concerned that the passed values from the main program were assigned to string pointers (char *) rather than character arrays. BASIC programmers have difficulty here because it seems like one type of value is being assigned to another type of variable. True, we are dealing with two different types of *variables*, but both contain the same type of values; namely, character strings. As mentioned before, C treats character arrays and character pointer variables as one and the same in many operations. Therefore, there is no problem whatsoever in assigning a string pointer the total value of a character array, or vice versa. Remember the strcpy function, which copies one character string found in one variable to another variable? This function may be used to pass the contents of a character array to a string pointer, or vice versa. With this in mind, this new version of the left function should not seem so unusual.

```
main()
{

        char *b, *d;

        d = "MICROPROCESSOR";
        left(b, d, 5);

        printf("%s\n", b);

}
left(a, c, i)
char a[], c[];
int i;
{

        int x;

        for (x = 0; x <= i - 1; ++x)
                a[x] = c[x];

}
```

In this program, we can treat character array c as we might treat string array C$ in BASIC and assume that each element of this array contains a single sequential character in the word MICROPROCESSOR. The *for* loop is entered and the value of x is used to determine the array position. Notice that this loop counts from 0 rather than 1, since a[0] and c[0] represent the first element position in each character array. Since i is assigned the total number of characters to be passed rather than the array element positions, we must subtract 1 from the value of i to be in sequence with the loop count, which begins at 0 rather than 1. Counting from 1 to 5 gives us five different numbers. Counting from 0 to 4 also gives us five different numbers, with 0 being the first. Each time the loop cycles, the array element position is stepped by 1 and the five elements contained in c are passed to a.

Returning to the discussion of incremental operators, the following program is the same as the first two (operationally), but uses incremental operators to assign the array positions.

```
main()
{

    char *b, *d;

    d = "MICROPROCESSOR";
    left(b, d, 5);

    printf("%s\n", b);

}
left(a, c, i)
char a[], c[];
int i;
{

    int x, y, z;

    y = z = 0;

    for (x = 1; x <= i; ++x)
        a[y++] = c[z++];

}
```

This example is more complex than it needs to be, but this is done to demonstrate the use of "following" incremental operators. Two new integer values are declared. Each is assigned a value of 0 by the $y = z = 0$; sequence.

This time, the loop count begins at 1 and counts up to the value of *i*. Character arrays *a* and *c* now use the values of *y* and *z* to determine positions. On the first cycle of the loop, both *y* and *z* are equal to 0. Therefore, the character at position c[0] is passed to a[0]. However, as soon as the value of 0 is used, the *following* incremental operators cause each variable to be stepped by 1. Therefore, on the next pass, *y* will be equal to 1, as will *z*. There might be a tendency to omit the *z* variable altogether and use:

a[y++] = c[y++];

This looks logical at first until you look a bit closer. On the first pass of the loop, a[y++] names the 0 element position in character array *a*. However, as soon as the value of 0 is used (in *y*), the value of *y* is stepped by 1. Therefore, when we come to c[y++], *y* is now equal to 1. This routine, then, would assign to the 0 element position of *a* the character found in the 1 element position of *c*. On the next pass of the loop, *y* would be equal to 3, since the c[y++] step incremented *y* again. To pull this off effectively, we have to have two variables, as shown in this program.

Incremental operators, when used with character string pointers, allow us to effectively initialize some shortcuts that you will see time and again in C programs. These shortcuts are not very easy for the beginner to understand without the proper background.

The following program is my version of the strcpy function that copies one variable value to another variable. I have represented the strcpy function here as strcp( ) to avoid confusion (in the compiler) with strcpy. This is done even though both work identically.

```
main()
{

    char *b, *d;

    d = "MICROPROCESSOR";
    strcp(b, d);

    printf("%s\n", b);

}
strcp(a, c)
char *a, *c;
{

    while ((*a++ = *c++) != '\0')
        ;

}
```

In C, the compiler creates an array of characters containing the characters of the string. It then terminates the character sequence with the null character represented by backslash 0 (\0). This null character is a signal that the end of the string sequence has been reached. Most functions that manipulate character strings or process them in some way do so until the null character is reached. The strlen function is an example of this; it reads the number of characters in a string. It does this by counting characters up to the point where the null character is intercepted. At this point, the counting process stops. The null character is *not* counted as part of the string.

This program uses the strcp function, which says that each position in *a* is equal to each position in *c* until the null character (\0) is reached. When the null character is intercepted, the loop is exited and control is returned to the main program. This might be best stated by saying that "as long as *a* is not equal to the null character, it is equal to the character found at the current position in c."

One other shortcut comes to mind here. All the *while* statement does is test for a condition of non-zero. This applies whether it's testing the value of two integers, pointers, or whatever. In BASIC, we may use the terminology of "WHILE tests for a *false* condition." The WHILE loop cycles until a false condition is detected. In C, the *while* statement does the same thing, but a false return is a zero return. A true return is a non-zero return.

Now, the null character is a zero. Therefore, it's not at all necessary to say "copy *c* to *a* as long as you don't receive a null character." The following program is just like the previous one, except any reference in the *while* line to the null character is deleted.

```
main()
{

    char *b, *d;

    d = "MICROPROCESSOR";
    strcp(b, d);

    printf("%s\n", b);

}
strcp(a, c)
char *a, *c;
{

    while (*a++ = *c++)
        ;

}
```

The function in this program operates exactly like the last one did, but we've shortened programming time simply by using fewer characters. Within the *while* loop, each character in *c* is copied to *a* until the null character is reached. The loop then terminates and control is returned to the main program.

I hope this discussion clears up some of the mysteries surrounding C. As in BASIC, there are many different ways to write a particular program operation. Programming efficiency often dictates the "pruning" of source programs to the smallest size possible. This is great as far as execution is concerned, but is often difficult for the beginner who's trying to learn a new language by viewing these source programs.

To again illustrate the relationship between character pointers and character arrays, the following program uses the strcp function with character arrays.

```
main()
{

    char *b, *d;

    d = "MICROPROCESSOR";
    strcp(b, d);

    printf("%s\n", b);

}
strcp(a, c)
char a[], c[];
{

    int x, y;

    x = y = 0;

    while (a[x++] = c[y++])
        ;
```

HEADER FILES

This section might have better been named "What to do with your functions after you've written them." Beginners often ask, "Is it necessary to type in my personalized functions with each and every program I write?" The answer is absolutely not. Undoubtedly, as you progress in C, you will develop a number of functions that address your own particular programming needs.

The best thing to do is combine all of these functions in a single file. This can be done by using your Line Editor (EDLIN in IBM DOS) to write all of your functions once they have been tested in actual programming environments. You do not call main( ) at anytime in such a file. Simply start out with the name of the first function just as if you were including it at the end of a program. When the first function is complete, follow it with the rest, again using the same format. When you are finished, you will have one entire file that contains nothing but C language functions. Let's assume the name of the file is "func.h." The ".h" designation can be used to indicate that this is a "header" file, so called because these files are typically included ahead of main( ) in any C language program that uses them.

We have already discussed one header file briefly. This is a standard header file called "stdio.h." This is an abbreviation for "standard input/output header file." It was previously mentioned that a C function is separate from a C program. C functions are called from C programs. While all of the previous examples in this book placed the functions at the end of the programs, there is no reason whatsoever why they cannot be included at the beginning, prior to the call to main( ). It doesn't make any difference where the function is positioned as long as it's outside of the executable program. When the call is made within the program, the function will be accessed.

Now, we have a file named func.h which contains personalized functions; let's assume that this file contains the left function discussed earlier. Assume also that a program is to be written that will call the left function. Here's how it should be written:

```
#include  <func.h>
main()
{

    char *a, *b;

    b = "COMPUTERS";

    left(a, b, 4);

    printf("%s\n", a);


}
```

You won't see the left function here, but, fortunately, the compiler does because the function is contained in the file named func.h. The preprocessor definition or inclusion is #include. This works similarly to #define, in that it is replaced by the entire contents of the file func.h. This is done just as though the entire contents of this file were typed into the program. During the compilation process, the contents of func.h are compiled along with your source program. For this reason, most header files are fairly short and include functions that are similar in nature. This might include a group of functions that process character strings. Another header file might contain functions that perform high-level mathematics. It's best to keep these files as short as possible and confine them to a certain processing area, because they will add size to your compiled programs. One header file might contain ten different functions, but only one of those functions may be used by the program doing the calling. Nevertheless, all of the other functions found in that file will be compiled. The only way to choose specific functions is to type them into your program, as discussed previously, or to make up header files that contain only single functions. The latter is quite laborious, and header files shouldn't take up too much space if designed according to operation.

Using the Lattice C-Compiler, it will be necessary for you to #include stdio.h when you wish to call functions like putchar, getchar, and others that deal with standard input/output and filekeeping. Technically, these are not functions (at least not in the Lattice C-Compiler), but macros that use the #define preprocessor directive. Your header files may also contain macros as well as functions, so feel free to use either.

The Lattice C-Compiler also contains a header file named conio.c, which is an abbreviation for "console input/output." This file contains functions such as *getch*, *putch*, and others. If you call any of these functions without also including the conio.c header file, your compiler probably won't issue an error message, but your linker will. The operation manual that accompanies your compiler will indicate which calls require the inclusion of header files. Be warned also that some header files will call other header files. This means that both files must be available on diskette. Again, your manual is the best source for this type of information.

The format I have used with the #include preprocessor directive is pretty much standard. However, this directive may also be used in the format of:

#include "header file name"

This is acceptable with the Lattice C-Compiler and should be with most others, but it always pay to check for such formatting in the operations manual.

You might also take note of the fact that with many compilers, you may compile your header file to arrive at an object code file. This file may then be linked with your compiled C language program (also in object code by this time) using your program linker.

SUMMARY

Normally, much of the type of discussion at the end of this chapter is relegated to the front portions of other books on C programming. I have chosen to "slip it in" during the discussion on functions because I feel that at this point the reader is better able to grasp these "basics," which are only basic if you have the proper base in C. The C programming language may seem a bit strange in the way it handles character strings, but this "weirdness" becomes a great attribute to handling the characters that make up strings once the proper background is obtained.

One of the prime beauties of C is the flexibility that can be had in writing your own personalized functions. Those that were discussed in this chapter border on the simple, but they do teach valuable lessons in proper program structuring. Remember, any program you can write in C can, in its entirety, be named a function. All you have to do is remove the main( ) opener and replace it with the function name and the list of arguments it will receive. This "program," then, can be called from another program as a function.

ASSIGNMENTS

1. Write a function that will mimic the RIGHT$ function in Microsoft BASIC.
   Hint: You must step the variable containing the value to be passed through its character positions until the starting one designated has been reached. Use strlen minus the number of characters to be passed to obtain the offset from the first character.
2. Write a function that will mimic the MID$ function in Microsoft BASIC.

C LANGUAGE FILEKEEPING

My first ideas about this book did not include the intention to write a chapter on filekeeping. Many will say this is not a subject appropriate for persons who are just getting acquainted with C. However, you will eventually want to write some filekeeping programs, so this chapter is included to at least give you some starting pointers.

This chapter may be thought of as a general overview of *elementary* filing programs in C. It does not delve deeply into this subject, but it does give you the starting criteria. C language filekeeping is better left to a complete text on the subject, because there are so many ins and outs and possibilities. C is a very efficient filekeeping language. File programs in C tend to be fairly short in comparison with other languages. Unfortunately, the operations that are taking place in most efficient programs are often masked from the student due to the shortcuts that are offered. It is hoped that this chapter will explain things on a level that can be appreciated and fully understood by the reader who is going from BASIC to C.

The purpose of any filekeeping program is to allow the operator to quickly name and open a diskette file. This really involves the origination of a file. After this point, it is necessary to be able to write information to the file, close it, and then open it again (posssibly at a later time) in order to read the information back. File processing can involve the order in which information is placed in a file (upon its creation) or the order in which it is read back from the file and displayed on the monitor screen.

C LANGUAGE FILE FUNCTIONS

While filekeeping programs can and do utilize nearly all of the functions found in C, there is a small group of functions that relate directly to filekeeping.

Many of these are necessary to open, close, read, and write information to a file. This chapter will discuss many of these functions, showing their general use. You will also find some functional programs that further demonstrate their uses. It should be pointed out that many of the functions used in file-keeping are macros. A macro may be thought of as a substitution for a number of combined functions that have been used to write a subroutine. These macros use established C language functions in such a way as to produce an entirely new function. It is not necessary to know how this is done, only that these macro substitutions are contained in the stdio.h header file, a standard part of nearly every C compiler.

   FOPEN: The fopen function is used to open a buffered file. Its basic format, as will be witnessed in most filekeeping programs, is:

```
fp = fopen (name, mode);
```

In this case, *fp* is a file pointer. When the fopen function executes, the file *name* and location will be identified by *fp*. The type of access under which the file is opened is determined by *mode*. In C, the mode may be one of three lower-case letters, "r", "w", or "a". In every case, these three letters must be lower case and must be inserted enclosed in quotation marks. The read mode is identified by "r". This means that the file is open for read only. Information may be pulled from the file and then processed. If the file which is opened for this type of access does not exist, a NULL will be returned to *fp*. The write mode is specified by "w." When a file is opened in this manner, information is written to the file. If a file, which does not already exist on diskette, is opened in write mode, an attempt is made to create this file. If the diskette is full or write-protected, NULL will be returned to *fp*. If a file, which already exists on diskette, is opened for write mode, its contents are completely erased. In order to add information to an already existing file, "a" is used to indicate the file is to be opened in append mode. If the named file does not already exist, it will be created under the stipulations discussed for write mode. When the file is opened, any additional information will be added to the end of the information already existing in the file.

   When opening a file using fopen, the file pointer (*fp* in this example) must be declared as such using the FILE declaration. Both the file name and mode may be declared as character strings, as in: char *name; char *mode;. Programs are usually handled in this manner when the name of the file and the mode is to be input via the keyboard. The two examples show how a program would be initially set up to open a file:

```
char *name;
char *mode;
FILE *fp;
fp = fopen (name, mode);
```

or

FILE *fp;
fp = fopen ("FILER", "w");

Both of these program setups will do exactly the same thing, assuming that the file is to be named FILER, and that it is to be opened in write mode ("w"). In the first example, the name and mode variables will be assigned in the program. In the second example, the actual file name and the mode were inserted directly. In opening files, it is necessary to check the file pointer (fp) for a NULL, which is returned when an opening is unsuccessful. The value of NULL is defined in the header file stdio.h. NULL will be returned anytime an opening error occurs. This may be generated if an invalid mode was specified, the file was not found (read mode only), the file could not be created, or too many files were already open. On most systems, no more than 16 files can be opened using fopen.

FCLOSE: The fclose function is the opposite of fopen. It closes a buffered file. When a call is made to fclose, the processing of the file is completed, and all related resources are released. If the file is being written, upon executing fclose, any data that is accumulated in the buffer is written to the file before closing. The buffer associated with the file block is freed. In C language, fclose is usually called automatically for all open files when a program calls the exit function or when the main() program returns. Exit functions are often used to terminate a program run whenever a NULL is returned to the file pointer or if another type of error should occur. While there are many automatic calls to fclose, it is still good programming practice to include this function in any program that opens a disk file. Fclose returns two values upon execution. In many systems, a 0 is returned for successful closing and a −1 if there is some reason why the file cannot be closed. The format in which this function is used is most often:

fclose (fp);

where *fp* is the file pointer. It may also be used to test for an error, as in:

int ret;
FILE *fp;
ret = fclose (fp);

An *if* statement would then be used to test for the value of *ret*, which would either be 0 (close completed) or −1 (error).

GETC: The getc function gets a character from a file that has already been opened for read mode. In the Lattice C-Compiler, the getc function is implemented as a macro that is part of the stdio.h header file. It returns a value of – 1 when an end-of-file error is detected.

FGETC: This function is not implemented as a macro and may be used in place of getc. Since this is a true function, fgetc is often used in place of the corresponding macro in the event that a lot of calls are made and the programmer is concerned about the memory used in the macro expansions. The macro is more efficient time-wise, because it saves the function call; but the function is more efficient space-wise, since its code is present in the program only once. From a programming standpoint, getc and fgetc may be used interchangeably.

PUTC/FPUTC: These functions/macros are the opposite of getc/fgetc. Both put a single character to the indicated file, as in:

```
FILE *fp;
char c;
int r;
r = fputc (c,fp);
or
r = putc (c,fp);
```

Variable *r* is equal to the character if sent successfully. If not, it is equal to EOF (defined in stdio.h).

FGETS: The fgets function gets an input string from a file. This string encompasses all of the characters up to the point where a newline (\n) is encountered or when the specified string length has been read. The format is:

```
fgets (name, string length, fp);
```

or

```
p = fgets (name, string length, fp);
```

In the first example, *name* is the file name, *string length* is the length of the character string to be returned, and *fp* is the pointer to the file itself. In the second example, *p* is a character string which serves as the returned string point. Variable *P* is NULL if an end-of-file or error is detected.

GETS: The gets function works in a similar manner to fgets, but the file it reads is always the standard input (stdin), which is the keyboard buffer. There is no string length parameter, and the standard input is assumed. The gets function is normally used to collect information from the keyboard buffer, which is later written to the opened diskette file. Its format is:

```
gets(x);
```

or

```
p = gets(x);
```

In each case, x is previously defined as a character string. In the second example, p is again the returned string pointer.

FPUTS/PUTS: The puts and fputs functions bear the same similarity as gets and fgets. They are both the opposite of these previous functions. Each puts an output string to a file. Using puts, the file is the standard output (stdout), or more simply, the monitor screen in most cases. The fputs function puts its information to a named file using a file pointer. The format for using these functions is:

```
FILE *fp;
char *x;
puts(x);
or
fputs(x,fp);
```

In these examples, x is a character string to be written to a file. Variable *fp* is a file pointer used only with fputs. You will notice that the format for puts and fputs is almost identical to the one for gets and fgets, save for the fact that there is no string length designator in either. In the case of puts, a file pointer is not necessary since the standard output is assumed.

CHARACTER TYPE MACROS

In *The C Programming Language* by Kernighan and Ritchie, seven character type macros were described. These were isalpha, isupper, islower, isdigit, isspace, toupper, and tolower. All of these are included in the Lifeboat Associates Lattice C-Compiler, but many others are available with this compiler as well. The discussion below outlines each of the available macros, including those that are more or less standard in most compilers and those that are also made available in the Lattice C-Compiler. Portions of this discussion are reprinted from the *Lattice 8086/8088 C Compiler Manual* from Lifeboat Associates.

The character type header file, called "ctype.h" on most systems, defines several macros that are useful in the analysis of text data. Most allow the programmer to determine quickly the type of a character; that is, whether it is alphabetic, numeric, punctuation, and so on. These macros refer to an external array called "_ctype," which is indexed by the character itself, so they are generally much faster than functions that check the character against a range or discrete list of values. Although ASCII is defined as a 7-bit code, the "_ctype" array is defined to be 257 bytes long, so that valid results are obtained for any character value. This means that a character with the value 0xb1, for instance, will be classified the same as a character with the value 0x31. Programmers who wish to distinguish between these values must test for the 0.80 bit before using one of these macros. Note that "_ctype" is actually indexed by the character value plus one; this allows the standard EOF value (-1) to be tested in a macro without yielding a nonsense result. EOF yields a zero result for any of the macros. It is not defined as any of the character types.

Here are the macros defined in the character type header file "ctype.h." Note that many of these will evaluate argument side effects, such as function calls or increment or decrement operators. Don't forget to include "ctype.h" if you use any of these macros; otherwise, the compiler will generate a reference to a function of the same name.

isalpha(c)	non-zero if c is alphabetic, 0 if not
isupper(c)	non-zero if c is uppercase, 0 if not
islower(c)	non-zero if c is lowercase, 0 if not
isdigit(c)	non-zero if c is digit, 0 if not
isxdigit(c)	non-zero if c is a hexadecimal digit, 0 if not (0-9, A-F, a-f)
isspace(c)	non-zero if c is white space, 0 if not
ispunct(c)	non-zero if c is punctuation, 0 if not
isalnum(c)	non-zero if c is alphabetic or digit
isprint(c)	non-zero if c is printable (including blank)
isgraph(c)	non-zero if c is graphic (excluding blank)
iscntrl(c)	non-zero if c is control character
isascii(c)	non-zero if c is ASCII (0-127)
iscsym(c)	non-zero if valid character for C identifier
iscsymf(c)	non-zero if valid first character for C identifier
toupper(c)	converts c to uppercase, if lowercase
tolower(c)	converts c to lowercase, if uppercase

Note that the last two macros generate the value of "c" unchanged if it does not qualify for the conversion.

These macros are extremely useful, since they can allow you to differentiate between certain types of file data information. For example, the isdigit macro can be used to allow only numerical information contained in a file to be eventually output to the monitor screen. The reverse is true of isalpha. When this is used, only alphabetic characters will be referenced. All but the last two of these macros seek for a specific class of characters (alphabetic, numeric, space, hexadecimal, graphic, and so on). Just as each may be used to screen characters that have been pulled from a file and allow them to be passed to another program portion that will display them on the monitor or write them to another file, they may also be used to prevent the characters they detect from being passed on to the display functions. These macros are invaluable for highly complex types of file processing, since each responds in one way—not to a certain character but to a certain class of character.

ADDITIONAL FILE FUNCTIONS

The Lattice C-Compiler is rich in highly specialized functions and macros that address filekeeping. In order for this text not to be terribly dependent on one compiler alone, the author has attempted to discuss all functions and macros that are considered to be common to the original language as described in *The C Programming Language*. Any obvious deviations from this major reference source have been identified as such.

At the earliest stage of learning to program in C, chances are your first program involved the simple process of printing your name on the screen. The printf function was used in a manner similar to:

```
printf ("name\n");
```

There is a similar function common to C that does basically the same thing, but instead of sending the output quantity (name) to the screen, this new function sends it to a designated file. The fprintf function generates a formatted output to the designated file. Its format is:

```
fprintf (fp, cs,arguments);
```

Here, *fp* is the file pointer; *cs* is a control string (which may also be designated in quotation marks and in direct mode), and *arguments* make up the variables that match the format control string designator. The format designator must be specified in lower case. These are the same designators you may be more accustomed to using with printf (that is, d, s, f, and so on). For example, the following program lines could be used to print the name Bob to the file identified by file pointer *fp*:

```
fprintf (fp, "Bob\n");
fprintf (fp, "%s", arg);
```

The second example assumes that variable arg has previously been designated a character string and assigned a value "Bob."

An error detecting macro, which is useful for general purposes including end-of-file or any other type of error, is *ferror*. This is a macro that generates a non-zero value if the indicated condition is true for the specified file. If an error occurs, the value is non-zero, zero if no error. In a program, this macro might be used as follows:

if (ferror(fp))
printf("File Cannot Be Opened\n");

STRING UTILITY FUNCTIONS

String utility functions are a group of functions in C that perform many of the most common string manipulations. These functions all work with sequences of characters terminated by a null byte, which is the C definition of a character string. These are especially useful in measuring the length of strings, copying one string to another, comparing two strings, and so on. These string utility functions are able to be used in processing character strings from file in much the same way that the character type macros were used to aid processing of individual characters in files.

STRLEN: The strlen utility function is basically the same as the LEN function in BASIC. It returns the length of a character string. It is common practice in C to terminate each line of a file with a null character, or terminator (\0). Most compilers automatically link this null terminator to the end of a newline character. When using strlen, the number of bytes in the string are counted up to the null terminator. The terminator itself is not included in the count. The standard format for this function is:

length = strlen(x);

where length is an integer variable and x is the character string. The number returned to length will be the number of bytes (characters) in the string prior to the null terminator.

STRCPY: The strcpy function copies one string to another. Its standard format is:

strcpy(to,from);

In this example, "to" is a character string pointer indicating the string onto which the second string is to be copied. In this case, "from" is also a character string pointer indicating the source string that is to be copied onto variable to. The strcpy function moves the null-terminated source string to the destination string. This function does not get a length parameter, so all of the source string is copied unconditionally.

STRCAT: This function concatenates strings, or more simply, adds one character string to the tail end of another. Its format is:

strcat (to,from);

Again, "to" is a string to which "from" is to be added. In this example, "from" is linked to the end of "to." "To" and "from" are both character string pointers. The result of the concatenated string is always null-terminated.

STRCMP: This is an extremely useful function that compares two strings on a byte-by-byte basis and returns an integer status indicating the result of the comparison. The standard format for the use of this function is:

x = strcmp (s,t);

where x has been defined as an integer, and s and t are character strings. If the two strings are identical, then x will be equal to 0. If the first string is less than the second string, a number that is greater than 0 will be returned. If the reverse is true, a number that is less than 0 will be returned.

It can be seen that while C is considered to be a "small" language, it is fairly rich in functions that are designed to do a tremendous amount of work regarding file processing. It is not necessary that you understand exactly how to use each of the functions or macros outlined in this chapter, only that you understand what their purpose is. The functions and macros outlined are by no means the full extent of all processing functions and macros available with the Lattice C-Compiler or most other C compilers. These are the ones, however, that will be used quite often. If you're in doubt as to the purpose of any of these functions or macros, please review this section before moving on to the following pages.

Now that the basics behind the C programming language and how it relates to filekeeping have been discussed, it is time to provide specific program examples. Rather than displaying an entire filekeeping program in C, I have chosen to build several filekeeping programs a few lines at a time. For the most part, each of these examples is a completely functioning program, even though they will later be used as elements for more comprehensive programs. If you have the facilities, you are encouraged to input each of these "little" programs and then run them on your computer. By discussing programs as a series of building blocks, I believe your understanding will be enhanced and at a later time, you will be able to look at a complex program and visually pull out the little programs of which it is made.

CREATE AND OPEN A FILE FOR WRITE

Before a file can be opened, it must first exist. Fortunately, the fopen function in the C programming language set will automatically create a file (if possible) when fopen is called for either the write ("w") or for append ("a"). If you fopen a file which already exists, for write the original file will be completely erased. Again, fopen will create a file if the "w" or "a" mode is used, unless the diskette is file-protected or there is no remaining storage space. In every case, the read, write, and append designations (r, w, a) must be specified in quotation marks and lower-case letters.

Figure 10-1 shows a complete program that will open (and create) a diskette file named cfile. This program uses the write mode, as specified by the lower-case w contained in quotation marks. This program does not write information to the file, but it does open it up in a way that will allow it to receive information should the additional program lines be added to allow this transfer. Notice that this file is #included at the beginning of the program. As always, main() begins the executable portion of the program. Every C program must have a main() at some point. This usually invokes other functions to perform its job, some of which come from libraries and others from the program into which it has been included. The opening brace encloses the statements that make up the file-opening function when coupled with the closing brace. Remember that in C, each program consists of a combination of functions that you write using the functions contained in the original language set. The first line of the function portion of the program, FILE *fp;, is a declaration stating that fp is a file pointer. The second line states that fopen returns a pointer to fp. This pointer is to the FILE, cfile. Enclosed within parens following fopen is the name of our file in quotation marks. This is followed by a comma and then again in quotation marks and lower-case letters, the mode under which the file is opened. In this case, a w is used to indicate that the file is opened under write mode. If the diskette does not contain a file already named cfile, this file will be created. If the diskette does already contain a file by this name, the contents of that file will be completely erased. Following the closing brace, execution terminates.

This simple program is a fully functioning program in itself, although it

```
#include <stdio.h>
main()
{

    FILE *fp;

    fp=fopen("cfile","w");
}
```

Figure 10-1

accomplishes nothing from a practical standpoint. It does open a file named cfile on diskette, but it writes nothing whatsoever to that file even though it was originally opened in write mode. However, this simple program will later be added to larger programs to develop a fully functioning filekeeping system.

In order to open a file, it is necessary for some variable to be defined as the file pointer. In this case, the variable is fp. To do this, the FILE declaration is used. This declaration is part of the stdio.h file, which was #included at the beginning of the program. The actual call to open the file is handled by the second line.

OPEN AN EXISTING FILE FOR READ

Now that you have opened (and created) a file for write, it is time to open an existing file in read mode. Figure 10-2 shows this program, which is identical to the one shown in Figure 10-1, with the exception that the original w has been replaced with a lower-case r. If your diskette contains a file named cfile, this program (Figure 10-2) will open it for the purpose of reading its contents. If such a file does not already exist, it will not be created by this program, and NULL will be returned to fp. There is no sense in discussing this program any further, as the rest of its contents act exactly as the matching contents in Figure 10-1.

At this point, it should be understood that any filekeeping program designed to read and write information to a diskette file must contain the line:

#include ⟨stdio.h⟩

Each program must also contain the FILE declaration and the file pointer variable. This variable must be preceded by the asterisk (*). Finally, any filekeeping program must contain the fopen function, which will specify the name of the file and the mode under which it is opened. These are the

```
#include <stdio.h>
main()
{

        FILE *fp;

        fp=fopen("cfile","r");

}
```

Figure 10-2

essential components of beginning a filekeeping program. The programs discussed thus far would equate to programs in BASIC that perform the same functions as follows:

10 OPEN "cfile" FOR OUTPUT AS #1

and

10 OPEN "cfile" FOR INPUT AS #1

or

10 OPEN "O", #1, "cfile"

and

10 OPEN "I", #1, "cfile"

The two sets of BASIC programs displayed here are various ways of opening files for write and for read when using IBM BASIC or MS BASIC. You will notice a similarity here when considering filekeeping in both languages. In BASIC, when a file is opened for output or append, it is created (written to diskette) if no such file exists. In the former mode, if a file does exist by that name, its contents are erased. In the append mode, the new information is added to the end of the present file's contents, assuming that file has previously been created. A further comparison can be made when files are opened in read mode (C language) or for input (BASIC). In both cases, if the file does not already exist, a NULL or error message is returned, depending on the language in which the program is written. In neither case will a file be created using the input or read mode.

ERROR MESSAGES

As is the case of any good program, it is necessary to build in prompts in the event that something the program is instructed to do cannot be done. The first and second examples in Figure 10-3 are identical, save for the fact that in the first the file is opened for write, while in the second it is opened for read. In both cases, the call to fopen the file is contained in an if-statement line. In Example A in Figure 10-3, the second line within the braces states in plain English, "If something goes wrong when the attempt is made to fopen cfile, then return NULL to file pointer fp." When null is returned, the printf line displays the error message:

ERROR: FILE cannot be opened.

```
#include <stdio.h>
main()
{

        FILE *fp;

        if ((fp = fopen("cfile","w")) == NULL){
          printf("ERROR:File cannot be opened.\n");
          exit(0);
        }

}


main()
{

        FILE *fp;

        if ((fp = fopen("cfile","r")) == NULL){
          printf("ERROR:File cannot be opened.\n");
          exit(0);
        }

}
```

Figure 10-3

At this point, the program is terminated due to exit(0);. On the other hand, if NULL is not returned to fp, the file will be opened in write mode as usual. The same set of events occurs in Example B, although if NULL is not returned, cfile will be opened for read mode. In Example A, a NULL might be returned if the diskette were write-protected or if its memory storage space were full. In the second example (B), a NULL would be returned if the file named in the if-statement line did not exist.

A FUNCTIONING WRITE FILE

As was previously mentioned, this chapter will slowly build a working file-keeping program based upon small building blocks or functions which in themselves are fully executable. Figure 10-4 shows an expansion of the previous programs that results in a filekeeping routine which will not only open a file for write mode but will also allow you to write information to the file.

First, it is necessary to establish a character variable that will serve to hold the information to be written to the file. In this case, the variable is named "buffer," which is quite descriptive, since this may be thought of as

```
#include <stdio.h>
main()
{

        char buffer[512];
        FILE *fp;

        if ((fp = fopen("cfile","w")) == NULL){
         printf("ERROR:File cannot be opened.\n");
         exit(0);
        }

        printf("Enter text to be written to file.\n");

        gets(buffer);

        fputs(buffer,fp);
}
```

Figure 10-4

the buffer to hold your keyboard input to be later transferred to diskette. This buffer is designed to hold a maximum of 512 characters. This figure is specified in brackets following the char buffer line in the program.. The next four lines were taken directly from the program in Figure 10-3A. Variable fp is designated as a file pointer, while the if-statement line opens the file in the write mode. Again, NULL will be returned if the file cannot be opened. An error message will be printed and the program terminated (exit) should NULL be returned.

Assuming that the file is properly opened, the printf line will display a prompt on the monitor screen telling you to enter text to be written to the file. The next line uses gets to place this information in the buffer. At this point, fputs is used to place the information contained in buffer in the file indicated by file pointer fp. Again, gets reads the information from the keyboard and places it in the character array named buffer. This array can hold a maximum of 512 characters. The information contained in this array is dumped to the diskette file by fputs. The gets function automatically pulls from the keyboard, so all that is needed is to include the name of the array in parens. The fputs function must contain in parens the name of the array or location from which to retrieve information and also the file pointer to indicate the file to which the array contents are to be written.

Figure 10-5 shows a sample program run. The top line is the screen

```
Enter text to be written to file.
This is an example of text to be written to a file.
```

Figure 10-5

prompt. The second line is the information that is typed in. Upon pressing the Enter key, this line was written to diskette. The program then terminates. If you run it again, however, any new information entered will not be added. Rather, the information already contained in the file will be entirely erased and will be replaced by any new input. This is due to the fact that the file is opened in write mode. To add information, it must be opened in append mode. This can easily be accomplished by changing the *w* in the if-statement line to a lower-case *a*. More on this later.

A FUNCTIONING READ FILE

Now that a program has been successfully built that will write information to the file, it is necessary to write one that will read information from this file. Shown in Figure 10-6, the same basic program is used, but a few changes have been made to allow for the input of the file name, the retrieval of information from the file, and the printing of it on the screen. Again, an array named buffer is established to hold a maximum of 512 characters. The file pointer fp is set up using FILE. The next line displays a prompt on the monitor screen indicating that the file name should be entered. The gets function is used to retrieve the file name from the keyboard and enter it into the array. Array name buffer now represents the file name.

The if-statement line is identical to the previous program, save for the

```
#include <stdio.h>
main()
{

        char buffer[512];
        FILE *fp;

        printf("Enter file name.\n");

        gets(buffer);

        if ((fp=fopen(buffer,"r")) == NULL){
          printf("ERROR: File cannot be opened.\n");
          exit(0);
        }

        fgets(buffer,512,fp);
        printf("%s",buffer);
}
```

Figure 10-6

fact that the buffer is used to represent the file name rather than the name itself. Also, the file is opened in read mode.

The fgets function is used to retrieve data from the file represented by buffer. This data can be up to 512 characters in length, while the file name carried in the buffer is located by pointer fp. The buffer array now contains up to 512 characters read from the file. To display information on the screen, printf is used. In this case, a conversion character represented by %s indicates that the characters read from buffer represent a string. These characters will be printed until a null character is reached or until the number of characters indicated by the array size has been reached. In this case, the first line of any file read by the program will be printed on the screen. Since this line will be terminated by a null character, the operation will stop at this point.

Figure 10-7 shows an alternate way of writing this program. The only change is near the bottom. Here, a *while* loop is formed. This allows fgets and printf to constantly retrieve and write information to the screen until the file has ended. The first program will write only a single line of file text to the screen, whereas the second program will display the entire file. Figure 10-8 shows a sample run and the complete file listing when reading cfile, which was established earlier using a program to write data to a file.

All of the programs presented up to this point are programs that are complete in themselves and should perform as described when input to your machine. The previous examples have shown how single programs, which in

```
#include <stdio.h>
main()
{

        char buffer[512];
        FILE *fp;

        printf("Name of file to list:\n");

        gets(buffer);

        if ((fp = fopen(buffer,"r")) == NULL){
          printf("ERROR:File cannot be opened.\n");
          exit(0);
        }


        while (fgets(buffer,512,fp))
            printf("%s",buffer);
}
```

Figure 10-7

```
Name of file to list:
cfile
This is an example of text to be written to a file.
```

Figure 10-8

C are really simple functions, are combined to offer more complex programs. You have been taken from the extremely simple program that opened the file for read or write to similar programs that do basically the same thing but indicate whether or not the file was successfully opened. Finally, all that went before was combined with a few new lines to provide an extremely simple but more or less complete program to open a file for write and allow you to write data to it or open a file for read and display the file contents on the screen. Admittedly, the programs presented are very limited in scope, since even the most complex ones allow for data to be written in the form of one line only. However, these programs serve as excellent examples of how complex filing programs are initially set up and the order in which the steps of this process take place.

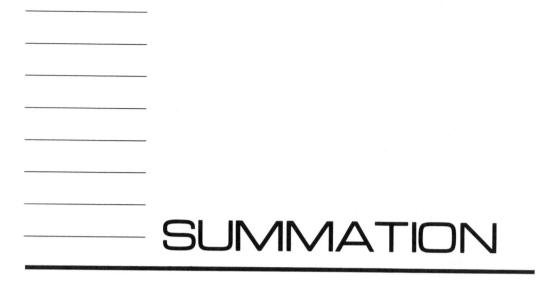

SUMMATION

This text was never intended to discuss *all* of what C has to offer. Rather, it is an introductory tutorial and basic reference guide aimed directly at the reader who is making the transition from BASIC to C. The text has discussed most of the oft-used functions that are of special significance to the beginner. The more elaborate C language availabilities, such as structs, unions, register variables, and so on have not been included here, nor have the many functions that address memory management. Still, C is a small language, and, with the proper base, these new elements can quickly be learned and mastered.

Hopefully, the information presented in this book will allow the beginner to effectively write simple to moderate level programs in C. More importantly, this data should provide an adequate base to allow the reader to appreciate and understand the higher-level information that is presented in other texts. At this juncture, C should not seem so strange, especially since you can now reference the BASIC language with its C language counterparts.

In summary, *Going from Basic to C* was designed to remove some of the mysteries about C and give the BASIC programmer the basic information needed in order to develop further and faster in C. It is hoped that the reader may use this information as a springboard for becoming versatile in writing C-language programs by building on a current knowledge of BASIC.

INDEX